Life

STUDENT'S BOOK | BEGINNER

NATIONAL
GEOGRAPHIC
L E A R N I N G

HELEN STEPHENSON

JOHN HUGHES

PAUL DUMMETT

Australia · Brazil · Mexico · Singapore · United Kingdom · United States

Contents

Pronunciation	Listening	Reading	Speaking	Writing
word stress questions	introductions phone numbers	a description of two people an article about international phone calls from New York	introductions a quiz greeting people	text type: an identity card writing skill: capital letters (1)
we're, they're *isn't, aren't* *be*: questions and short answers plural nouns syllables	a description of a place a conversation about a holiday	a description of photos of a trip a conversation about a holiday a quiz about holiday places	holiday photos on holiday general knowledge	text type: a form writing skill: capital letters (2)
possessive *'s* linking with *in* intonation	a description of a family from Mexico a conversation about a family from Iraq a description of good friends	a description of a family from Scotland an article about important days	my family people and things celebrations around the world	text type: a greetings card writing skill: contractions
th /ð/ linking with *can*	a description of Astana tourist information	describing places a description of two famous towers an article about time zones	locations famous places days and times	text type: a text message writing skill: *and*
can/can't *have/has* numbers	a profile of Yves Rossy an interview with a robot expert people talk about their interesting things	an article about robots and people a blog about technology	my abilities my things my favourite object	text type: an email writing skill: *but*
do you ... ? *likes, doesn't like* intonation	a description of a sport in South Africa an interview with a man about sport	an article about sport a profile of a TV presenter an article about street food	a sports survey a puzzle food	text type: short messages writing skill: punctuation and sentence structure

Pronunciation	Listening	Reading	Speaking	Writing
intonation in questions sentence stress	a description of the Holi festival interviews about hobbies with friends	an article about a day in China an article about the seasons of the year	my partner and I a survey about hobbies activities in different seasons	text type: a profile writing skill: paragraphs
-s and -es verb endings /s/ and /z/	an interview about a man's job an interview about an unusual school	an article about jobs on the London Underground an article about a job in tiger conservation	jobs things we usually do anmals	text type: an email writing skill: spelling: double letters
there are I'd like, We'd like	four people talking about travel a conversation about a trip to Cape Town	an article about things in people's suitcases an article about a trans-Siberian trip	things in my suitcase hotels travel tips	text type: travel advice writing skill: because
was/were weak forms sentence stress	a profile of Ayrton Senna a radio programme about people we remember	a quiz about 'firsts' in exploration an article about the first people in the American continents	dates and events people in my past who was he/she?	text type: an email writing skill: expressions in emails
-ed regular past simple verbs did you … ? didn't	a story from Timbuktu, Mali an interview with a woman from New Orleans	an article about an unusual discovery a story about an adventure in Madagascar	true or false? last week and year one day last week	text type: a life story writing skill: when
going and doing would you … ?	three people talk about weekend activities a description of a family in Indonesia	a short message about next weekend an article about helping people at the weekend	my photos next weekend a special weekend	text type: a thank you note writing skill: spelling: verb endings

Life around the world – in 12 videos

Unit 6 At the market

Meet people at a market in an English city.

Unit 10 Old computers

Find out about computers from the 1980s.

USA

UK

Unit 8 The London Tube

Meet a Tube driver at work.

Unit 3 Chinese New Year in London

Find out about street celebrations.

Unit 4 Where's that?

A video quiz about four cities.

Unit 12 A day in the life of a lighthouse keeper

At the lighthouse at Cabo Polonio, Uruguay.

Uruguay

Unit 9 The people of the reindeer

Find out about the life of the Sami people.

Unit 11 True stories

Four people tell their stories. Are they true or false?

Russia

Unit 5 What's your favourite gadget?

Two people talk about their favourite gadget.

Nepal

Unit 1 My top ten photos

A photographer talks about his favourite photos.

Kenya

Unit 7 The elephants of Samburu

Find out about elephants in the Samburu National Park.

Australia

Unit 2 A holiday in Australia

On holiday with two friends.

**UNIT 1
HELLO**

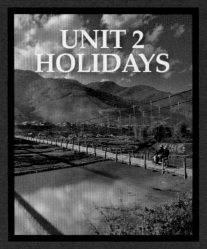

**UNIT 2
HOLIDAYS**

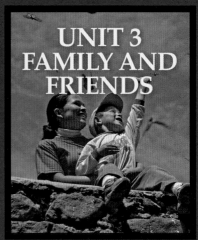

**UNIT 3
FAMILY AND
FRIENDS**

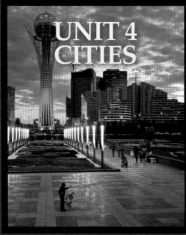

**UNIT 4
CITIES**

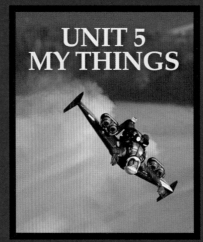

**UNIT 5
MY THINGS**

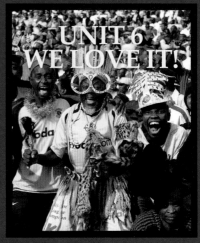

**UNIT 6
WE LOVE IT!**

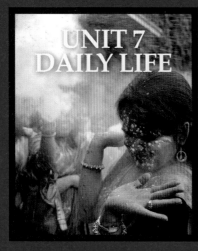

**UNIT 7
DAILY LIFE**

**UNIT 8
WORK AND
STUDY**

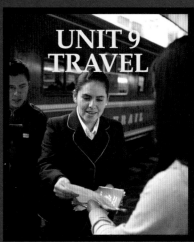

**UNIT 9
TRAVEL**

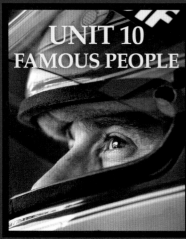

**UNIT 10
FAMOUS PEOPLE**

**UNIT 11
TRUE STORIES**

**UNIT 12
THE WEEKEND**

David Doubilet in the
Pacific Ocean, Australia

FEATURES

1 ▶1 Look at the photo. Listen and read.

Hello! I'm David.

2 ▶1 Listen and repeat.

3 Say your name.

Hello! I'm _____ .

4 Work in pairs.

Hello! I'm Dani.

Hello! I'm Lee.

1a People

Listening

1 ▶2 Listen and read.

1
D: Hello. I'm David.
M: Hi. I'm Mireya.
D: Mireya Mayor?
M: Yes.

2
D: Hi! I'm David Doubilet.
M: Hello.
D: Oh! You're Mireya!
M: Yes. I'm Mireya Mayor.

3
D: Hello. I'm David Doubilet.
M: I'm Mireya.
D: Mireya?
M: Yes. M–I–R–E–Y–A.
D: Hi. Nice to meet you.

N A T I O N A L   G E O G R A P H I C   P E O P L E

David Doubilet

Mireya Mayor

Vocabulary the alphabet

2 ▶3 Listen and repeat.

Aa	Bb	Cc	Dd	Ee	Ff	Gg
Hh	Ii	Jj	Kk	Ll	Mm	Nn
Oo	Pp	Qq	Rr	Ss	Tt	Uu
Vv	Ww	Xx	Yy	Zz

3 ▶4 Say the letters. Listen. Write the letters.

A	B	F	I	O	Q	R
H	C	L				
	D					

4 ▶5 Listen and repeat.

a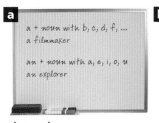
a + noun with b, c, d, f, ...
a filmmaker

an + noun with a, e, i, o, u
an explorer

board

b

book

c

chair

d

desk

e

door

f

window

5 Work in pairs.
Student A: Say the letters.
Student B: Say the word.

C–H–A–I–R   chair

yes

6 ▶6 Listen. Write the names.

1 _____
2 _____
3 _____
4 _____

7 Work in pairs.
Student A: Spell your name.
Student B: Write the name.

Grammar *be*: *I* + *am*, *you* + *are*

▶ BE: I + AM, YOU + ARE	
I'm	*Alex.*
You're	*Mireya.*

(I'm = I am, You're = You are)

Now look at page 158.

8 Write *I* or *You*.

S: Hello. _____ 'm Sandra.
K: Hi!
S: Oh! _____ 're Kim!
K: Yes, _____ 'm Kim Smith.

Speaking my life

9 ▶7 Listen and read. Speak to other students.

Hi, I'm Carlos.

Hello. I'm Sonia. Nice to meet you, Carlos.

Nice to meet you, Sonia.

1b People and places

PEOPLE AND PLACES

1 This is Katya. She's from Moscow. It's in Russia. Katya is Russian.

2 This is Lukas. He's from Cape Town. It's in South Africa. Lukas is South African.

Reading

1 ▶ 8 Read and listen.

2 Write the words in the table.

	Photo 1	Photo 2
Name	Katya	
Country		
Nationality		South African

Vocabulary countries and nationalities

3 ▶ 9 Write the words in the table. Listen and check.

> Egyptian   Mexico   Spanish   the United States

	Country	Nationality
1	Brazil	Brazilian
2	Egypt	....
3	Italy	Italian
4	....	Mexican
5	Russia	Russian
6	South Africa	South African
7	Spain	....
8	the United Kingdom	British
9	....	American
10	Vietnam	Vietnamese

4 Pronunciation word stress

▶ 10 Listen and repeat the countries. Copy the stress.

● ●
Brazil

● ● ●
Mexico

Grammar *be: he/she/it + is*

▶ **BE: HE/SHE/IT + IS**

He		from Russia.
She	**is**	Russian
It		in Russia.

(He's, She's, It's = He is, She is, It is)

Now look at page 158.

5 Look at the photos. Write *He is*, *She is* or *It is*.

1 Tran

2 Juan

3 Krishnan

4 Marina

1 Tran is from Hanoi. _____ in Vietnam. _____ Vietnamese.
2 Juan is from Seville. _____ in Spain. _____ Spanish.
3 Krishnan is from Chicago. _____ in the United States. _____ American.
4 Marina is from Milan. _____ in Italy. _____ Italian.

6 Write the information. Show your partner.

	You
Name	
Place	
Country	
Nationality	

7 Tell the class about your partner.

This is Kira. She's from France. She's French.

Vocabulary numbers 1–10

8 ▶ 11 Write the numbers (1–10). Listen and repeat.

0 zero	___ four	___ eight
___ one	___ five	___ nine
___ two	___ six	___ ten
___ three	___ seven	

9 ▶ 12 Look at the table in Exercise 3. Listen. Say the country.

'seven'   *Spain*

10 ▶ 13 Look at the table in Exercise 3. Listen. Say the number.

'Spain'   *seven*

Speaking ⟨ my life ⟩

11 ▶ 14 Work in pairs. Do the quiz. Listen and check.

Baseball is Russian.

False. It's American.

QUIZ   TRUE OR FALSE?

around the world

01 Baseball is Russian.

02 Pasta is from South Africa.

03 Jaguar is British.

04 Flamenco is from Italy.

12 Work in pairs. Write an 'Around the world' quiz. Write four sentences. Test the class.

1c Phone calls from New York

Reading

1 Read *Phone calls from New York* on page 15. <u>Underline</u> four countries.

2 Read again. Write the names.

1 _____ is a teacher.
2 _____ is Mexican.
3 _____ is from Canada.
4 _____ is Indian.

Listening

3 ▶ 15 Listen to Anne-Marie. Tick (✓) the phone number (a or b).

a 718 730 7121   b 718 760 7101

4 ▶ 16 Listen to Nelson. Write.

1 work phone number _____
2 home phone number _____

Grammar *my, your*

> ▶ **MY, YOUR**
>
> *What's **your** phone number?*
> ***My** phone number is 718 760 7101.*
>
> Now look at page 158.

5 Write *my* or *your*.
R: Hi. ¹ _____ name's Ramon.
N: Hello. I'm Nelson.
...
N: Ramon, what's ² _____ phone number?
R: ³ _____ work number is 917 275 6975.
N: Thanks. What's ⁴ _____ mobile number?
R: It's 917 398 9763.
N: Thanks.

6 Work in pairs. Ask and answer questions.

mobile
number

work
number

home
number

Vocabulary greetings

7 ▶ 17 Write the expressions in the correct places. Listen and repeat.

Bye	Hello

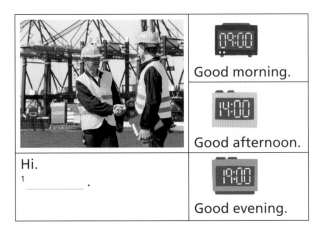

	Good morning.
Hi. 1 _____ .	Good afternoon.
	Good evening.

| Goodnight.
[23:00] | |
| Goodbye.
2 _____ . | See you later. |

8 ▶ 18 Listen to two conversations. Write the numbers (1 or 2).

Bye, Anne-Marie. _____
Fine, thanks. And you? _____
Good morning, Ramon.
  How are you? _____
I'm OK. _____
Goodnight, Ramon. _____

9 ▶ 19 Listen and repeat the conversations.

Speaking   my life

10 Practise the conversations in Exercise 8 with your class.

> *Good afternoon, Vicente. How are you?*

PHONE CALLS FROM NEW YORK – THE TOP TEN COUNTRIES

▶ 20

AUSTRALIA

5
India

AFRICA

9
Italy

ASIA

EUROPE

6
France

8
Germany

2
the
United
Kingdom

1
Canada

NORTH AMERICA

● New York

4
Mexico

7
Jamaica

3
Dominican
Republic

10
Brazil

SOUTH AMERICA

My name's Nina. I'm a student. I'm in New York. My family is in India. I'm Indian.

My name's Anne-Marie. I'm in New York. I'm a student. I'm Canadian. My family is in Canada. Canada is the number 1 country for international phone calls from New York.

My name's Ramon. I'm a doctor. I'm in New York. I'm Mexican. My family is in Mexico.

My name's Nelson. I'm Brazilian. I'm a teacher. I'm in New York. My family is in Brazil.

1d What's this in English?

Vocabulary in the classroom

1 ▶ 21 Listen. Write the words.

1

2

3

4

5

6

7

8

2 ▶ 22 Listen to the words from Exercise 1 and repeat.

3 Work in pairs. Point to a photo in Exercise 1. Ask and answer questions.

What's this in English?

It's a _____ .

Can you spell it?

Yes. _____ – _____ .

Thanks.

Real life classroom language

4 ▶ 23 Listen. Look at the classroom language box.

5 ▶ 23 Listen again. Write T (teacher) or S (student).

▶ **CLASSROOM LANGUAGE**

Good afternoon, everyone. *T*
Sit down, please.
Open your books.
Look at page six.
Sorry I'm late.
Can you repeat that, please?
I don't understand.
Can you spell it, please?
What's this in English?
Do Exercise seven at home.
See you next time.

6 Pronunciation questions

a ▶ 24 Listen and repeat the questions from the classroom language box.

b Look at the audioscript on page 182. Practise conversations 4, 6 and 7.

7 Work in pairs. Write the words. Practise the conversations.

1 T: Good morning. _____ I'm late.
   S: That's OK. Sit down, _____ .

2 S: Can you _____ that, please?
   T: Yes. Look at _____ ten.

3 T: Look at the photo.
   S: I don't _____ .

my life ▶ INTRODUCTIONS ▶ A QUIZ ▶ GREETING PEOPLE ▶ **CLASSROOM LANGUAGE**
▶ AN IDENTITY CARD

1e My ID

Writing an identity card

1 Look at the ID card and find:

   1 the name of the company
   2 the name of the visitor

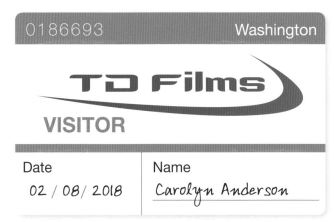

2 Writing skill capital letters (1)

a <u>Underline</u> the capital letters on the ID card.

b Write these words in the table.

Brazil	Nelson Pires
Brazilian	Rio de Janeiro
Portuguese	

a city	London
a country	the United Kingdom
a language	English
a name	Alex Treadway
a nationality	British

c Rewrite the sentences with the correct capital letters.

   1 santiago is in chile.
   2 maya davis is a teacher.
   3 I'm chinese.
   4 He's from tokyo.
   5 She's from canada.
   6 I speak french.

3 Complete the ID cards with the information. Use capital letters.

1 dublin
    sean booth

2 american
    cathy johnson

3 paris   bangkok   sydney
    jan sastre

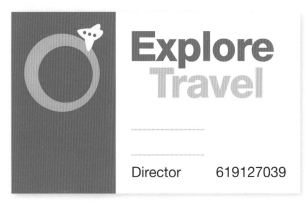

4 Write your ID card.

5 Work in pairs. Check your partner's card. Check the capital letters.

1f My top ten photos

A woman and a baby from Mongolia

a **climber**
(noun)
/ˈklaɪmə/

fantastic
(adjective)
/fænˈtæstɪk/

a **fisherwoman**
(noun)
/ˈfɪʃəwʊmən/

happy
(adjective)
/ˈhæpi/

a **lion**
(noun)
/ˈlaɪən/

an **ocean**
(noun)
/ˈəʊʃən/

a **river**
(noun) /ˈrɪvə/

a **water buffalo**
(noun)
/ˈwɔːtə ˌbʌfələʊ/

a **whale**
(noun)
/weɪl/

Before you watch

1 Work in pairs. Look at this photo. Complete the information about Tom.

I'm   is   my   name's

Hi. My ¹ .... Tom. ² .... a photographer. This ³ .... my top ten – ⁴ .... favourite *National Geographic* photos – of people and places.

2 ▶ 25 Look at the word box on page 18. Listen and repeat the words.

While you watch

3 🎥 1 Watch the video. Tick (✓) the correct column.

photo	a man	a woman	people	an animal / animals
1		✓		
2				
3				
4				
5				
6				
7				
8				
9				
10				

4 Work in pairs. Compare your answers from Exercise 3.

Photo number two is a man.

Yes, I agree.

5 🎥 1 Watch the video again. <u>Underline</u> the correct country.

Photo 1   Nepal / India
Photo 2   China / Nepal
Photo 3   Mongolia / Vietnam
Photo 4   the United States / Canada
Photo 5   Brazil / Bangladesh
Photo 6   Canada / New Zealand
Photo 7   Australia / the United States
Photo 8   Mozambique / South Africa
Photo 9   Namibia / Kenya
Photo 10 Kenya / South Africa

6 🎥 1 Read the sentences. Write true (T) or false (F). Watch the video again and check.

Photo 1   The photographer is Alex Treadway.
Photo 2   The man is from the Himalayas.
Photo 3   The woman is happy.
Photo 4   The fisherwoman is from Alaska.
Photo 5   This is a photo of water buffalo.
Photo 6   The whale is in the ocean.
Photo 7   The climber is Jimmy Chin.
Photo 8   The photo is in Africa.
Photo 9   The photographer is from National Geographic.
Photo 10 Tom says 'This photo is my favourite.'

7 🎥 1 Watch the video again. What's your favourite photo?

After you watch

8 Complete the information about three of the photos.

Photo 1 is by Alex Treadway. The woman is ¹ .... Nepal in the Himalayas. ² .... Nepalese.

Photo 7 ³ .... by Jimmy Chin. This ⁴ .... Kate Rutherford. ⁵ .... 's from the United States. She's a climber.

Photo 10 is people ⁶ .... Namibia in Africa. ⁷ .... by Chris Johns. ⁸ .... a *National Geographic* photographer.

9 Write about your favourite photo.

Grammar

1 Complete the sentences with these words.

I'm	you're	he's	she's	it's	it's

1 Hi. My name's Rosa. _____ from Brazil.
2 This is David. _____ a teacher.
3 I'm from Ottowa. _____ in Canada.
4 A: I'm Alain.
   B: Oh! _____ my teacher!
5 Marina is from Italy. _____ Italian.
6 Duc is from Hanoi. _____ in Vietnam.

2 Complete the sentences with *my* or *your*.

1 I'm Susana. What's _____ name?
2 Hello. I'm _____ teacher.
3 Hi. _____ name's Samir.
4 What's _____ phone number?
5 Open _____ books at page four.
6 This is _____ phone number: 718760.

3 ≫ MB Make true sentences.

My name's _____ . I'm from _____ .
I'm _____ .

I CAN
talk about people and places (*be*)
use *my* and *your* correctly

Vocabulary

4 Write the names of the objects.

1 _____   2 _____

3 _____   4 _____

5 _____   6 _____

5 Complete the countries. Write the nationalities.

1 V__ t n__ m
2 __ g__ p t
3 S__ t h__ f r__ c__
4 R__ s s__
5 B r__ z__ l
6 S p__ n

6 ≫ MB Work in pairs. Take turns.
Student A: Write five numbers. Say the numbers to your partner.
Student B: Write the numbers. Check.

7 ≫ MB Work in pairs. Take turns.
Student A: Write five words. Say the letters of the words to your partner.
Student B: Write the words. Check.

I CAN
talk about things in the classroom
talk about countries and nationalities
greet people
count to ten
say the alphabet and spell words

Real life

8 Match 1–5 with a–e to make exchanges.

1 Sorry, I'm late.
2 What's this in English?
3 This is a table.
4 Can you repeat that, please?
5 See you next time.

a Yes. Work in pairs.
b Can you spell it, please?
c Bye.
d It's a computer.
e That's OK. Sit down, please.

9 Work in pairs. Practise the exchanges in Exercise 8.

I CAN
understand classroom instructions
talk to my teacher and my classmates about the lesson

Unit 2 Holidays

Two people on a bridge in Mai Chau

FEATURES

1 ▶ 26 Look at the photo. Choose the correct option (a–c). Listen and check.

a This is in Brazil. It's a beach. It's evening.
b This is in France. It's a city. It's night.
c This is in Vietnam. It's a river. It's morning.

2 ▶ 27 Look at these two places. Listen and repeat.

the sea
an island
a beach

a mountain
a city
a lake

3 Complete the sentences with words from Exercise 2.

1 Bangkok is a _____ . It's in Thailand.
2 Titicaca is a _____ . It's in Bolivia and Peru.
3 Copacabana is a _____ . It's in Brazil.
4 Everest is a _____ . It's in Nepal.

4 Write four sentences about places. Read your sentences to your partner.

2a My holiday

MY HOLIDAY BLOG   by Laura   ▶ 29

THURSDAY
03 JAN

Today is Thursday. I'm in Tunisia. It's beautiful! It's evening. I'm with my
friends Brad, Andy and Jessica. We're on a beach. We're happy. Andy and
Jessica are Canadian. They're doctors. They're on holiday too.

Vocabulary days of the week

1 ▶ 28 Write the days of the
week in order. Listen, check
and repeat.

> Friday ~~Monday~~ Saturday
> Sunday Thursday Tuesday
> Wednesday

1 Monday

2 Work in pairs.
Student A: Say a day.
Student B: Say the next day.

Reading

3 Work in pairs. Look at the
photo. Choose the place (a–c).

a a city
b a beach
c a lake

4 Read *My holiday blog.* Find:

1 a day of the week
2 the name of the country
3 the names of the people

Grammar *be: we/they + are*

▶ BE: WE/THEY + ARE		
We They	are	in Tunisia. Canadian.

(We're, They're = We are, They are)

Now look at page 160.

5 Look at the grammar box. Underline *we're* and
they're in *My holiday blog*.

6 ▶ 30 Complete the sentences. Listen and check.

1 This is Jane. This is Paul. They _____ Australian.
2 I'm Meera. This is Suri. We _____ from India.
3 In this photo, I'm with my friend Jack. _____ 're
in Egypt.
4 Laura is with Brad, Andy and Jessica. _____
on holiday.
5 Monique and Claude are from France. _____
French.
6 I'm happy. My friend is happy. _____ happy!

7 Pronunciation *we're, they're*

a ▶ 31 Listen and repeat six sentences from Exercise 6.

b Work in pairs. Write sentences with *We're*. Read
your sentences to a new pair.

We're in Moscow.

Grammar *be*: negative forms

▶ BE: NEGATIVE FORMS		
I	am not ('m not)	happy. on a beach.
You	are not (aren't)	
He/She/It	is not (isn't)	
We/You/They	are not (aren't)	

Now look at page 160.

8 Look at the grammar box. What are the negative forms of *am*, *is* and *are*?

9 Read these sentences about the photo on page 22. Write true (T) or false (F). Correct the false sentences.

1 It's Wednesday.
   It isn't Wednesday. It's Thursday.
2 The friends aren't on a beach.
3 They're happy.
4 Andy and Jessica are from Tunisia.
5 Brad is in the photo.
6 Laura isn't in the photo.

10 Look at the photo for Saturday. Write these words in the blog.

| not | aren't | isn't | isn't |

11 Pronunciation *isn't*, *aren't*

a ▶ 32 Listen and repeat the sentences from Exercise 10.

b Write true sentences. Read your sentences to your partner.

> *We aren't on a beach.*

I'm	a student.
I'm not	a doctor.
	in a city.
	in a classroom.
You're	in Egypt.
You aren't	happy.
	on a lake.
We're	on a beach.
We aren't	on holiday
	from Morocco.

Speaking ⟨ my life ⟩

12 Work in groups. Show a photo to your group. Tell your group about your photo. Use *this is* and affirmative and negative forms of *be*.

> *This is a photo of my friends, Carlos and Enrique. We're in Egypt.*

MY HOLIDAY BLOG by Laura

SATURDAY 05 JAN

In this photo, we ¹_____ in Tunisia. We're in Morocco. It ²_____ a beach. It's the Sahara Desert. Andy and Jessica are on camels. Brad ³_____ on a camel. He's in a tent. I'm ⁴_____ in this photo.

2b Where are you?

Vocabulary numbers 11–100

1 ▶ 33 Write the numbers. Listen and repeat.

_11_	eleven
	twelve
	thirteen
	fourteen
	fifteen
	sixteen
	seventeen
	eighteen
_19_	nineteen

2 ▶ 34 Write the numbers in order. Listen, check and repeat.

eighty   fifty   forty
ninety   seventy   sixty
thirty   twenty

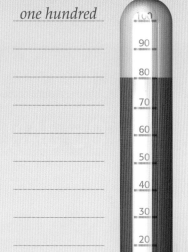

one hundred	100
	90
	80
	70
	60
	50
	40
	30
	20
ten	10
zero	0

3 ▶ 35 Look at the pictures (a–e). Listen and match.

1 _b_   2 _____   3 _____   4 _____   5 _____

a
TEMPERATURE: 16°C
HUMIDITY: 45%

08:32 Mon
4°C

LONDON
31°C

d
37°C

e
City	Temperature
Cape Town	23°C
Casablanca	29°C
Chicago	16°C
Copenhagen	11°C

4 ▶ 36 Look at the numbers in Exercise 3 again. Listen. Are the numbers the same – or different?

a 'It's thirteen degrees.'   **different**

5 ▶ 37 Write the numbers. Listen and check.

nineteen   six   thirty-five

1 It's _____ degrees in Oslo today. It's cold.
2 It's _____ degrees in Sydney today. It's hot.
3 It's _____ degrees in Lisbon today. It's warm.

6 Work in pairs. Look at the cities in Exercise 3. Talk about the temperatures. Use *hot*, *warm* and *cold*.

It's twenty-three degrees in Cape Town.   *It's warm.*

Reading and listening

7 Lorna is Australian. She's on holiday in Europe. Read the conversation. Answer the questions.

1 Where's Lorna?
2 Where's Greg?
3 Where are Kara and Ona?

8 ▶ 38 Listen. Choose the correct option.

Greg: Hi! Where are you now? Are you in ¹ *France / Italy*?

Lorna: Yes, I am. I'm in the Alps. It's beautiful!

Greg: Are you OK?

Lorna: No, I'm not. It's ² *two / thirty-two* degrees!

Greg: Wow! Is it ³ *cold / hot* in your hotel?

Lorna: No, it isn't. The hotel is nice.

Greg: It's ⁴ *thirty-six / sixteen* degrees in Sydney today.

Lorna: Oh! That's ⁵ *hot / cold*!

Greg: Are Kara and Ona in France?

Lorna: No, they aren't. They're on a ⁶ *beach / lake* in Morocco!

Greg: OK! See you on Friday.

Grammar *be*: questions and short answers

▶ BE: QUESTIONS and SHORT ANSWERS		
Am I		Yes, I am. No, I'm not.
Is she/he/it	OK? cold?	Yes, she/he/it **is**. No, she/he/it **isn't**.
Are we/you/they		Yes, we/you/they **are**. No, we/you/they **aren't**.

Now look at page 160.

9 Look at the grammar box. Look at the conversation in Exercise 8. <u>Underline</u> the questions.

10 Write the words in order.

1 you / OK / are / ?
Are you OK?
2 is / in France / Kara / ?
3 in Sydney / you and Paul / are / ?
4 in London / is / Greg / ?
5 Kara and Ona / in Morocco / are / ?
6 nice / your hotel / is / ?

11 Match the questions in Exercise 10 with the answers (a–f).

a Yes, they are.   d Yes, it is.
b No, he isn't.   e No, she isn't.
c Yes, I am.   f Yes, we are.

12 Pronunciation *be*: questions and short answers

a ▶ 39 Listen and repeat the questions and answers from Exercises 11 and 12.

b Work in pairs. Practise the questions and answers.

Speaking 〔my life〕

13 Work in pairs. You are on holiday. Have a telephone conversation with your friend.
Student A: Turn to page 153.
Student B: Turn to page 155.

2c A holiday quiz

Vocabulary colours

1 ▶ **40** Look at the colours. Listen and repeat.

black blue *brown*
green **orange** pink
red white *yellow*

2 Find six of the colours in the photos on page 27.

Reading

3 Find *a car* and *a bus* in the photos.

4 Read the quiz on page 27. Match the photos with four sentences.

5 ▶ **41** Work in pairs. Look at page 27 again. Write the words in the box in the correct sentences. Listen and check.

Grammar *a/an*

▶ A	AN
a + noun with *b, c, d, f, …* *a car*	*an* + noun with *a, e, i, o, u* *an island*

Now look at page 160.

6 Look at the grammar box. Write *a* or *an*.

1 Paris is _____ city.
2 _____ lion is _____ animal.
3 Gatwick is _____ airport.
4 Kilimanjaro is _____ mountain.

Grammar plural nouns

▶ NOUNS	
Singular	**Plural**
an airport	*airports*
a lake	*lakes*
a country	*countries*
a beach	*beaches*

Now look at page 160.

7 Look at the grammar box. Underline seven plural nouns on page 27.

8 Pronunciation plural nouns

a ▶ **42** Listen and repeat these nouns.

/s/	/z/	/ɪz/
lakes	cars	beaches
airports	countries	buses

b ▶ **43** Write the plural of these nouns. Listen and repeat.

a book   a desk   a student
a bag   a city   a hotel   a mountain
a language   a page   a place

9 Word focus *in*

Write the expressions in the correct place.

in Australia   in a car   in French
in a hotel   in Italian   in Moscow

1 in English _____
2 in Europe _____
3 in a classroom _____

Speaking my life

10 Work in pairs. Write four sentences – two true and two false. Use these words.

a city / cities   a country / countries
an island / islands   a lake / lakes

Lima and Santiago are cities in Mexico. Rome is a city in Italy.

11 Work in groups of four. Read your sentences. Say *true* or *false*. Correct the false sentences. Take turns.

Lima and Santiago are cities in Chile.

False. Lima is in Peru.

A Holiday Quiz

Australia   black   China
France   island   lakes
London   red

1 In London, buses are _____ .
2 In Hawaii, beaches are _____ .
3 Cuba is an _____ . In Cuba, cars are old.
4 In Iceland, the _____ are hot.
5 Lake Geneva is in two countries – Switzerland and _____ .
6 The Blue Mountains are in _____ .
7 Hong Kong, Shanghai and Beijing are cities in _____ .
8 Heathrow is an airport in _____ .

2d Here are your keys

Vocabulary car hire

1 ▶ 44 Listen and match 1–4 with a–d.

1 a car registration number
2 an email address
3 an address
4 keys

b 3 Park Street
Gateshead
NE2 4AG

c To: jamesp@national.org

d PT61 APR

2 Work in pairs. Take turns.
Student A: read an email address.
Student B: say the number (1–5).

1 smith23@hotmail.com
2 ryan.law@google.co.uk
3 barry@egg.com
4 smnrss@gmail.com
5 b.mark@me.com

3 Work in pairs. Ask your partner their address, email address and car registration number.

Real life personal information

4 ▶ 45 Listen to the conversation. Answer the questions.

1 Is the woman from Mexico?
2 Is she on holiday or on business?

5 ▶ 45 Listen again. Choose the correct option.

1 Car hire: *two days* / *three days*
2 Name: *Ms Lopez* / *Mr Lopez*
3 Email address: *mlopez@hotmail.com* / *mlopez@hotmail.com.mx*
4 Car registration number: *BD52 ACR* / *BD61 ATC*

6 Work in pairs. Look at the audioscript on page 183. Practise the conversation.

> ▶ **PERSONAL INFORMATION**
>
> What's your first name? / ... surname?
> Where are you from?
> I'm from Mexico City.
> What's your (email) address? / ... phone number?
> Is this your (email) address? / ... phone number?
> Here's my ID card.
> Here are your keys.
> Note: in email addresses we say *at* for @ and *dot* for '.'

7 Pronunciation syllables

a ▶ 46 Listen and repeat the words. Count the syllables.

holiday   ho – li – day = 3

address	car	email	evening	key
number	seventeen	surname	telephone	

b ▶ 46 Listen again. Underline the main stress in the words.

<u>ho</u>liday

8 Work in pairs. Practise the conversation with new information.

> *Good evening.*

> *Hello, I'm Mr Lopez.*

2e Contact information

Writing a form

1 Match 1 and 2 with the options (a and b).

  a a hotel online booking form
  b an internet profile

1

Enya Farrell

Call name: enya123

Mobile phone: 0795 157 963
Home phone: 00 44 161 8542
Email address: enya@bt.com
Country: UK
Contacts: 19

2

Title	Ms ⌄
First name	Enya
Surname	Farrell
Address	16 Liverpool Road
City	Manchester
Postcode	M23 9PL
Country	UK ⌄
Email address	enya@bt.com

2 What's your title? Is it Mr, Mrs or Ms?

3 Writing skill capital letters (2)

a Look at the information in form 2. <u>Underline</u> the capital letters.

b Rewrite this information with the correct capital letters.

  1 11 hill view   4 judd
  2 g12 3xt   5 mr
  3 glasgow   6 ryan

4 Complete the college registration form with the information from Exercise 3b.

🛡 REGISTRATION FORM

Title _____
First name _____
Surname _____
Address _____
_____
City _____
Postcode _____
Contact number *0733 489 145*
Email address *ryan@judd.co.uk*

5 Complete the online booking form with your own information.

Title	⌄
First name	
Surname	
Address	
City	
Postcode	
Country	⌄
Email address	

6 Check your form. Check your capital letters.

A holiday in Australia

A koala in a tree in Australia

Before you watch

1 Look at the photo on page 30. What's the animal? Where is it?

2 Look at the map of Australia. Count the states. Answer the questions.

1 Is Brisbane in South Australia?
2 Is Adelaide a city or a state?
3 Is Tasmania an island?

3 Key vocabulary

a Read the sentences. Match the underlined words (1–4) with the pictures (a–d).

1 <u>Kangaroos</u> are from Australia.
2 This is <u>the sun</u> in the morning.
3 <u>The sky</u> is blue.
4 We're in a <u>plane</u>.

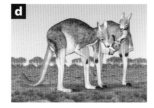

b ▶ 47 Listen and repeat the <u>underlined words</u>.

4 ▶ 48 Look at the word box. Listen and repeat the words.

While you watch

5 ◻2 Watch the video. Write at least five words. Read your words to your partner.

> sea   blue

6 ◻2 Watch the video again. Put these places in the order they are in the video (1–3).

a beaches b a city c the country

After you watch

7 Work in pairs. Test your memory. Ask and answer the questions.

1 What animal is in a tree?
2 What colour is the lizard?
3 What animals are in the sea?
4 Is the person in the sea a man or a woman?

8 Work in pairs. Write questions about South Australia with these words.

1 South Australia / beautiful / ?
2 the beaches / nice / ?
3 animals / amazing / ?
4 South Australia / a good place for a holiday / ?

9 Ask a new partner your questions.

> Is South Australia beautiful?

> Yes, it is.

> No, it isn't.

 birds (noun) /bɜːdz/

 a boat (noun) /bəʊt/

 the country (noun) /ˈkʌntri/

a dolphin (noun) /ˈdɒlfɪn/

 a lizard (noun) /ˈlɪzəd/

 a road (noun) /rəʊd/

 a seal (noun) /siːl/

Grammar

1 Complete the texts with the words. Then match the photo with Greg or Kara.

'm	isn't	not	we're

GREG: I'm in the mountains. I [1] _____ with my friends. We're in Canada. [2] _____ on holiday. I'm [3] _____ happy – the hotel [4] _____ nice.

are	aren't	isn't	they're	we

KARA: I'm in Brazil with my friends Jorge and Ana. [5] _____ Brazilian. I'm on holiday. Jorge and Ana [6] _____ on holiday. [7] _____ 're in Rio de Janeiro. The beaches [8] _____ beautiful. The sea [9] _____ cold – it's warm!

2 Write questions.

1 you / a student?
2 your teacher / American?
3 we / in Asia?
4 your friends / teachers?
5 this classroom / cold?
6 you / OK?

3 ▶▶ MB Work in pairs. Ask and answer the questions in Exercise 2.

4 ▶▶ MB Work in pairs. Look at the words and write the plurals. Take turns.
Student A: Say a word.
Student B: Say the plural.

1 airport _____
2 beach _____
3 bus _____
4 city _____
5 country _____
6 photo _____

I CAN	
ask and answer questions (*be*)	☐
use regular plural nouns	☐

Vocabulary

5 ▶▶ MB Work in pairs. Say the days in order. Take turns. Start with **Monday**.

6 ▶▶ MB Work in pairs. Take turns.
Student A: Say a number from 11 to 100.
Student B: Write the number.

7 Choose the correct colour.

1 My car is *red / orange*.
2 My phone is *blue / black*.
3 The mountains are *white / pink*.
4 The buses are *yellow / green*.
5 The lake is *brown / blue*.

I CAN	
say the days of the week	☐
count from eleven to one hundred	☐
say the colours of objects	☐

Real life

8 Complete 1–5 with these words. Then match 1–5 with a–e.

here's	holiday	name's	this	where

1 Good afternoon. My _____ Smith.
2 _____ my passport.
3 _____ are you from in Ireland, Mr Smith?
4 Are you on _____ here?
5 Is _____ your email address?

a Good afternoon, Mr Smith. What's your first name please?
b I'm from Dublin.
c No, I'm not. I'm on business.
d Thank you.
e Yes, it is.

9 Work in pairs. Practise the exchanges in Exercise 8.

I CAN	
ask for and give personal information	☐

Unit 3 Family and friends

A family in Mexico look at butterflies.

FEATURES

1 ▶ 49 Look at the photo. Listen and read.

This family is from Mexico. The people are Rosa, Lidia and Pablo. Rosa is the mother. Lidia is the daughter. Pablo is the son.

2 Write *Lidia, Pablo* and *Rosa*.

1 _____ is a boy.   3 _____ is a girl.

2 _____ is a woman.

3 Write *daughter* and *parents* in the correct place.

father & mother = ¹ _____

son   ² _____

4 Work in pairs. Write sentences about you with a family word. Read your sentences to your partner.

> *I'm a son.*
> *I'm a father.*

> *I'm a daughter.*
> *I'm not a mother.*

3a Families

The Murray family

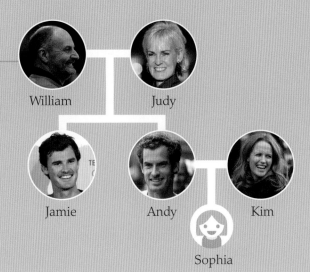

William   Judy

Jamie   Andy   Kim

Sophia

▶ 51

Andy Murray and Jamie Murray are top tennis players. Judy is their mother. She's a tennis player too. Their father is called William. He isn't a tennis player. Andy is married. His wife is called Kim. Sophia is a little girl. Her parents are Andy and Kim. The Murray family is from Scotland.

Vocabulary family

1 Look at the family tree. Which sport is this family famous for?

2 ▶ 50 Listen and repeat the family words.

brother	daughter	father	husband
mother	sister	son	wife

3 Write the correct words for the Murray family tree.

1 Andy and Jamie are ___brothers___ .
2 Andy and Kim are husband and
   _____ .
3 William and Jamie are father and
   _____ .
4 Kim and Sophia are mother and
   _____ .

Reading

4 Read about the Murray family. Write the names.

1 Their parents are William and Judy.
   _____ and _____
2 Their sons are Jamie and Andy.
   _____ and _____
3 Her mother is Kim. _____
4 His daughter is Sophia. _____
5 Her husband is Andy. _____
6 His brother is Jamie. _____

Grammar *his, her, its, our, their*

▶ **HIS, HER, ITS, OUR, THEIR**

*He's my father. **His** name's William.
She's my mother. **Her** name's Judy.
They're my sons. **Their** names are Jamie and Andy.
Our parents are Judy and William.
We're from a town in Scotland. **Its** name is Dunblane.*

Now look at page 162.

5 Look at the grammar box. Write *singular* or *plural*.

1 *her* and *his* = _____
2 *our* and *their* = _____

6 Write *her* or *his*.

1 This is Angela. _____ mother is Rose. _____ father is Jack.
2 This is Jamie. _____ mother is Judy. _____ father is William.
3 This is David. _____ son is Anton.
4 This is Jack. _____ daughters are Mary and Angela.
5 This is Susan. _____ brother is Stephen.
6 This is Andy. _____ parents are William and Judy.

7 Write *our* or *their*.

1 I'm Sam. My brother is Bill. _____ parents are Sue and David.
2 This is a photo of Lili and Jenna. _____ mother is my sister.
3 This is my family. _____ surname is Sanderson.
4 This is my sister and her husband. These are _____ children.
5 My brother and his wife are thirty. _____ son is five.
6 I'm Frank. My wife is Lisa. _____ daughter is two years old.

Listening

8 ▶ 52 Look at the photo and the conversation. Write *my*, *your*, *his* or *her*. Listen and check.

A: Is this a photo of [1] _____your_____ family?
B: Yes, it is.
A: Who's this?
B: She's [2] _____ sister. [3] _____ name's Heelan. It's her wedding.
A: OK. So is this [4] _____ husband?
B: Yes. [5] _____ name's Husham.
A: Is this [6] _____ daughter?
B: Yes. [7] _____ name's Nadia.
A: How old is she?
B: She's twelve years old.

9 Look at the answers. Complete the questions about the people in the photo with these words.

he	her	his	she	their	they

1 Where are _____ ?
  In Baghdad.
2 What's _____ name?
  Nadia.
3 What are _____ names?
  Husham and Heelan.
4 What's _____ wife called?
  Heelan.
5 How old is _____ ?
  Twelve years old.
6 Is _____ the husband?
  No. Husham is the husband.

Speaking my life

10 Work in pairs. Show your family photos to your partner. Ask and answer questions.

Who's this?

He's my brother.

3b Friends

Vocabulary people

1 Look at the photo of Ana. Complete the
information with four of the words.

| eyes | hair | old | short | tall | young |

My name's Ana. I'm twenty-one years
¹_____. My ²_____ are blue
and my ³_____ is brown. I'm not
⁴_____. I'm short. I'm a student at The
English Academy.

2 Put the words in the correct order to make
questions. Answer the questions.

1 colour / what / is / hair / your / ?
2 eyes / are / what / your / colour / ?
3 are / old / how / you / ?
4 tall / you / are / ?

Listening

3 ▶ 53 Listen to Ana. Match the names (1–3)
with the information (a–c).

1 Elisa   a her brother
2 Nuno   b her classmate
3 Prem   c her best friend

4 ▶ 53 Listen again. Complete the sentences.

1 Elisa's eyes are _____.
2 Elisa's hair is _____.
3 Nuno's eyes are _____.
4 Nuno's hair is _____.
5 Prem's eyes are _____.
6 Prem's hair is _____.

5 Work in pairs. Ask and answer questions
about three friends. Use the questions in
Exercise 2 with *his/her*.

*My best friends are
Luigi, Enzo and Paulo.*

How old is Luigi?

He's 19.

What colour are his eyes.

They're brown.

Ana

Elisa

Nuno

Prem

Grammar possessive 's

▶ **POSSESSIVE 'S**

Ana's eyes are blue.
Nuno's hair is brown.

Now look at page 162.

6 Look at the grammar box. Is this sentence true or false?

Possessive 's is the same as *his and her*.

7 Write sentences with the information.

1 Ana / Nuno / sister
   Ana is Nuno's sister.
2 Elisa / Ana / friend
3 Prem / Ana / classmate
4 Ana / eyes / blue
5 Prem / school / The English Academy
6 Ana / friends / Elisa, Nuno and Prem

8 Pronunciation possessive 's

a ▶ 54 Listen and repeat the sentences from Exercise 7.

b Make sentences about students in your class.

Marco's eyes are brown.

9 Read the sentences (1–2). Match 's with its uses (a–b).

1 Elisa's my best friend.
2 Elisa's eyes are brown.

a possessive *s*
b contraction of *is*

10 Read the sentences. Underline 's. Write *P* (possessive) or *C* (contraction).

1 What's this? ....
2 His car's red. ....
3 Jack's books are here. ....
4 Who's this? ....
5 Susan and Charlie are my brother's children. ....
6 This is my teacher's book. ....

Speaking my life

11 Work in pairs. Take turns.
Student A: Point to a photo. Ask *What's this?*
Student B: Answer.

What's this?

It's Anita's bag.

Anita

Jack

Lin

Eric

Claude

Krishnan

12 Ask and answer questions about your things.

3c Important days

Vocabulary months

1 ▶ 55 Write the months in order. Then listen, check and repeat.

April	August	December	February
January	July	June	March	May
November	October	September

1 January

2 Work in pairs. Take turns.
Student A: Say a month.
Student B: Say the number of days.

July   *thirty-one*

Reading

3 Work in pairs. Complete the sentences.

December   February   January   October

1 New Year's Day is in _____ .
2 Halloween is in _____ .
3 Christmas Day is in _____ .
4 Valentine's Day is in _____ .

4 Read *Important days*. Match (a and b) with two of the important days in the texts.

5 Read *Important days* again. Underline five months.

6 Work in pairs. Ask and answer the questions.

1 Is Chinese New Year in March?
2 Is Thanksgiving an American celebration?
3 Is the London Marathon for children?
4 Are the Oscars® in June?

7 Pronunciation linking with *in*

▶ 56 Listen and repeat the sentences.

1 It's in March.
2 They're in February.
3 Is it in London?

Grammar irregular plural nouns

> ▶ **IRREGULAR PLURAL NOUNS**
>
> a child → two **children**
> a man → three **men**
> a woman → four **women**
> a person → five **people**

Now look at page 162.

8 Look at the grammar box. Circle the regular plural nouns and underline the irregular plural nouns in *Important days* on page 39.

9 ▶ 57 Listen and repeat the words in the grammar box.

10 ▶ 58 Complete the sentences with these words. Read the sentences to your partner. Listen and check.

children   men   people   women

1 My _____ are boys.
2 Andy and David are the _____ in my family.
3 The _____ in my class are Spanish and Italian.
4 Rosa, Lidia and Ana are _____ in my class.

Writing and speaking ⟋ my life

11 Write three, four or five words from one of the texts on page 39. Work in pairs and tell your partner the words. Take turns.

American, families, November

12 Write sentences with your partner's words. Read your sentences to your partner. What's the important day?

It's American.

It's for families.

It's in November.

Is it Thanksgiving?

Important DAYS

a

b

▶ 59

1 Chinese New Year is a big celebration. It's in January or February. Chinese New Year is fun. Chinese people in different countries are happy.

2 Thanksgiving is an American celebration. Thanksgiving is for families. It's in November.

3 The London Marathon is a race. It's 42 kilometres. The London Marathon is for men and women from all over the world. It isn't for children. The London Marathon is a big celebration. It's in April.

4 Oscars® night is a celebration of films. Oscars® night is in Hollywood. It's in February. It's for American and international films.

3d Congratulations!

Vocabulary special occasions

1 Look at these words. Look at the photo and listen to a conversation. What's the special occasion?

a birthday	a new year
a new baby	a wedding

2 ▶ 60 Put the parts of the conversation (a–e) in order (1–5). Listen again and check.

a   Ah, she's lovely. What's her name?
b   Congratulations!   *1*
c   Hello, Juba.
d   It's Juba.
e   Thank you. We're very happy.

Real life special occasions

3 ▶ 61 Listen to three more conversations. Number (1–3) the occasions in Exercise 1.

4 ▶ 61 Look at the expressions for SPECIAL OCCASIONS. Listen again. Write the number of the conversation.

> ▶ **SPECIAL OCCASIONS**
>
> Congratulations!
> Happy Birthday!
> Happy New Year!
> I'm very happy for you.
> Here's a present for you.
> How old are you?

5 Pronunciation intonation

a ▶ 62 Listen and repeat the expressions for special occasions.

b Work in pairs. Look at the audioscript on page 184. Practise the three conversations.

Real life giving and accepting presents

6 Work in pairs. Match the special occasions (1–3) with the presents (a–c).

a    **b**   **c**

1   your friend's birthday
2   a new baby
3   your cousin's wedding

7 ▶ 63 Listen to the conversation. Tick (✓) the expressions for GIVING AND ACCEPTING PRESENTS.

> ▶ **GIVING AND ACCEPTING PRESENTS**
>
> **This is for** you / the baby.
> **That's** lovely / very kind.
> Thanks. / Thank you very much.
> You're welcome.

8 Work in pairs. Choose a special occasion. Practise the conversation from Exercise 7. Take turns.

> *Hi. This is for …*

my life   ▶ MY FAMILY   ▶ PEOPLE AND THEIR THINGS   ▶ CELEBRATIONS AROUND THE WORLD
     ▶ SPECIAL OCCASIONS   ▶ A GREETINGS CARD

3e Best wishes

Writing a greetings card

1 Writing skill contractions

a <u>Underline</u> the contractions in these sentences. What's the missing letter?

1 I'm Australian.
2 She's French.
3 It isn't my birthday.
4 What's your name?
5 It's beautiful.
6 Who's this?
7 They're my cousins.
8 When's the party?

b Find and <u>underline</u> four contractions in these messages.

> **1**
> Hi. I'm in London with my brother. It's his birthday on Monday. Where are you? Phone me!

> **2**
> Is it Mother's Day on Sunday?

> **3**
> Ingrid and Karl's wedding's in June. What's Karl's surname?

c Rewrite these messages. Use contractions.

> **1**
> Karin's birthday is on Friday. She is twenty-one. Her party is on Saturday.

> **2**
> Hi. I am twenty-five today. Come to my party! It is at my house.

> **3**
> Hi. What is Katya's address? Is it number 5 or 7? Thanks.

2 Read the messages. Answer the questions.

1 What's the occasion?
2 Who's the card from?
3 Who's the card to?

To Harry
Happy birthday!
Love and best wishes from
Katya and Bruno

To Diana
Thank you for our wedding present.
It's beautiful!
Best wishes from
Ingrid and Karl

3 Write messages for cards for a new baby and a birthday. Use some of these words. You can use some words more than once.

best wishes	birthday	congratulations
from	love	on	thank you	to
your		

4 Read the cards. Check the capital letters.

5 Work in pairs. Compare your cards with your partner's cards.

3f Chinese New Year in London

A dragon in a Chinese New Year celebration

Before you watch

1 Read about Chinese New Year. Complete the article with three of these words.

> animals   countries   family   February

Chinese New Year

Chinese people live in ¹ _____ around the world. New Year celebrations are in January or ² _____ . Chinese years are ³ _____ : tiger, dragon, horse, dog, etc. The Chinese New Year celebration in London is a big party.

2 Key vocabulary

a Read the sentences. Match the <u>underlined</u> words (1–3) with the pictures (a–c).

1 This work is <u>excellent</u>.
2 We're at a school <u>reunion</u>.
3 I <u>dress up</u> as Spider-Man.

b ▶ 64 Listen and repeat the <u>underlined</u> words.

3 ▶ 65 Look at the word box. Listen and repeat the words.

While you watch

4 ☐◀3 Watch the video. Tick (✓) the things you see.

dragons	streets
children	trees
dogs	fireworks

5 ☐◀3 Watch the video again. Match the people (1–3) with their words (a–c).

1 a boy
2 a man
3 a girl

a It's also a family reunion.
b Lots of people dress up in red.
c Absolutely excellent.

6 ☐◀3 Complete the sentences. Watch the video and check.

1 It's Chinese New Year. This celebration is in _____ .
2 We celebrate British New Year in _____ and then Chinese New Year.
3 It's traditional to give _____ .
4 In the _____ , people watch fireworks.

After you watch

7 Work in pairs. Test your memory. Write six things from the video. Compare with your partner.

8 Work in pairs. Translate the sentences from the video into your own language. Compare with your partner.

1 It's really great.
2 Red is the lucky colour for Chinese.

> a **beginning** (noun) /bɪˈɡɪnɪŋ/ start
>
> a **dog** (noun) /dɒɡ/
>
> **fireworks** (plural noun) /ˈfaɪəwɜːks/
>
> a **street** (noun) /striːt/

UNIT 3 REVIEW AND MEMORY BOOSTER

Grammar

1 Complete the sentences with these words.

her   his   our   their

1 This card is for Ellie and Greg. What's .... address?
2 A: Is that David's sister?
   B: No, it's .... friend.
3 This is my wife and these are .... three children.
4 A: Your baby is lovely! What's .... name?
   B: It's Elena.

2 Complete the sentences with the possessive form.

1 Look at the photo. This is ....
   (Jin / family)
2 This is ....
   (Sandra / car)
3 They're ....
   (Toni / keys)
4 This is ....
   (Diana / phone)
5 This is ....
   (Michael / passport)
6 They're ....
   (Enya / books)

3 »MB Work in pairs. Take turns.
Student A: Ask questions about the people and things in Exercise 2.
Student B: Cover the page. Answer the questions.

I CAN
talk about people and possessions (possessive adjectives and possessive 's)

Vocabulary

4 Match the words for men and women.

brother	daughter
father	grandmother
grandfather	mother
husband	sister
son	wife

5 »MB Work in pairs. Ask and answer questions about family. Take turns.

What's your ...'s name?

6 Choose the correct option.

1 My sister is tall and I'm *short / old*.
2 What colour are the baby's *eyes / hair*?
3 My children are *tall / young* – five and six years old.

7 »MB Work in pairs. Take turns.
Student A: Say a month.
Student B: Say the next month.

I CAN
talk about my family and friends
talk about months and ages

Real life

8 Put the words in order. Then match 1–4 with a–d.

1 you / present / a / here's / for / .
2 is / how old / he / today / ?
3 very / kind / is / that / .
4 the / is / wedding / when / ?

a is / eighteen / he / .
b much / thank / very / you / .
c in / is / July / it / .
d are / welcome / you / .

9 Work in pairs. Practise the exchanges in Exercise 8. Use contractions.

I CAN
talk about special occasions
give and accept presents

Evening in the city of Astana in Kazakhstan, Asia

FEATURES

1 Look at the photo. Find these things.

buildings   children   a garden   trees

2 Read the caption with the photo. Find the name of the city, the country and the continent.

3 ▶ 66 Read the sentences. Then listen and write true (T) or false (F).

1 Astana is the capital city of Kazakhstan.
2 The buildings in Astana are tall.
3 The buildings are a different colour at night.
4 Astana is a dirty city.

4 Work in pairs. Talk about your city, town or village.

I'm from Brasilia. It's in Brazil. It's modern.

Is it the capital?

Yes, it is.

4a In the city

Vocabulary places in a town

1 ▶ 67 Look at the words and pictures. Listen and number the words.

a bank	a market
a bus station	a museum
a café	a park
a car park	an information centre
a cinema	a train station

2 ▶ 67 Listen again and repeat the places.

3 Are the places in Exercise 1 in your town? What are their names?

> *The cinemas in my town are called the Phoenix and the Rialto.*

Reading

4 Look at the map. Find four places in London Street. Find one place in Exeter Street.

5 Read the comments about four places. Are the comments good or bad?

6 Read the comments again. Write the names of the places.

1 The _____ is new.
2 The _____ is popular.
3 The _____ is old.
4 The _____ is in Oxford Street.

a bank

b Transport Museum

c bus station

d Royal Café

e car park

f City Information Centre

g Roxy Cinema

h Central Market

i train station

j Green Park

The museum isn't very good. It's old. It's near the railway station.
Berta

This café is great! It's popular with students. It's next to a cinema.
Artem

Grammar prepositions of place (1)

▶ **PREPOSITIONS OF PLACE**

in   *next to*   *opposite*   *near*

Now look at page 164.

7 Look at the grammar box. Look at the comments. <u>Underline</u> the prepositions.

8 Read the sentences. Look at the map. Write true (T) or false (F).

1 The museum is in London Street.
2 The café is next to the cinema.
3 The park is near the information centre.
4 The market is opposite the cinema.

9 Look at the map. Choose the correct option.

1 The bank is *next to / opposite* the market.
2 The cinema is *in / near* London Street.
3 The car park is *near / next to* the museum.
4 The information centre is *next to / opposite* the bus station.
5 The bus station is *in / next to* the park.
6 The train station is *opposite / near* the museum.

10 ▶ 68 Listen to four conversations about places on the map. Write the number of the conversation (1–4) next to the places.

a bank ....
b car park ....
c information centre ....
d train station ....

11 ▶ 68 Listen again. Look at the map. Is the information correct?

Speaking my life

12 Work in pairs. Look at the audioscript on page 184. Practise the conversations from Exercise 10.

13 Work in pairs. Ask and answer questions about places on the map.

> Excuse me?
> Yes?
> Where's the market?

14 Work in pairs. Ask and answer questions about four places in your town.

> Where's the Coffee Pot café?
> I'm not sure!

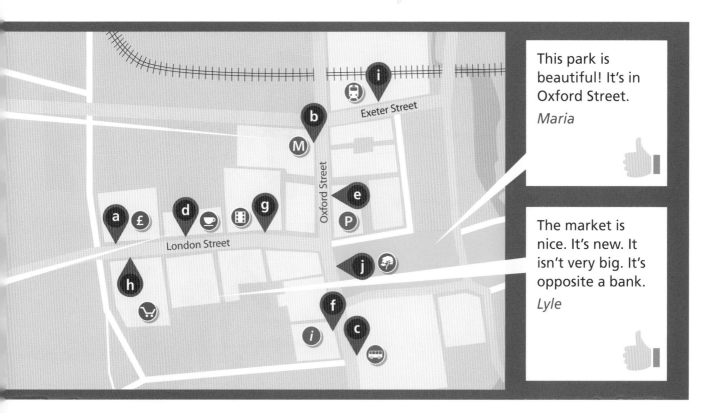

This park is beautiful! It's in Oxford Street.
Maria

The market is nice. It's new. It isn't very big. It's opposite a bank.
Lyle

4b Tourist information

Listening

1 ▶ 69 Listen to two conversations in a Tourist Information Centre. Number the parts of the conversations in order.

1 a Good morning.
  b Is **this** a map of the city?
  c Hi. *1*
  d No, it isn't. **That's** a map of England. **This** is a map of London.
  e OK. And where's the London Eye?
  f Yes, it's open every day.
  g Oh, yes. Is it open on Sunday?
  h It's near the River Thames … here it is.

2 a And bus timetables?
  b Good afternoon. Where are the timetables, please?
  c OK, thanks.
  d **Those** are bus timetables, next to the door.
  e Well, **these** are train timetables, here.

2 Work in pairs. Practise the conversations in Exercise 1.

Grammar *this, that, these, those*

▶ **THIS, THAT, THESE, THOSE**

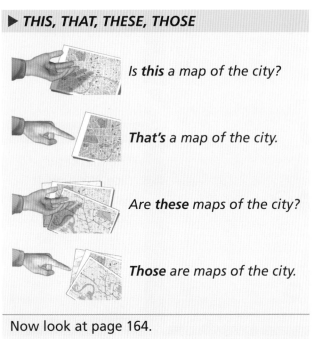

Is **this** a map of the city?

That's a map of the city.

Are **these** maps of the city?

Those are maps of the city.

Now look at page 164.

3 Look at the grammar box. Write *singular* or *plural*.

1 *this* and *that* are _____
2 *these* and *those* are _____

4 ▶ 70 Read the conversations. Write *this*, *that*, *these* and *those*. Listen and check.

1

Is _____ a train timetable?

No, it's a bus timetable.

2
Excuse me. Are _____ pens or pencils?

I'm not sure … Oh, yes. They're pencils. The pens are next to the maps.

OK, thanks.

3
Excuse me. Are _____ maps of London?

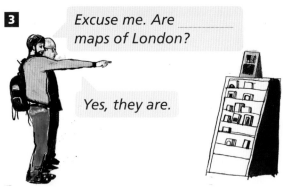

Yes, they are.

4
Is _____ guidebook in English?

Which guidebook?

The book next to you.

No, it isn't. It's in Spanish.

The Skytree

▶ 72

What is it?
It's a tower.

Where is it?
It's in Tokyo, Japan.
It's near Asakusa
Station.

When is it open?
It's open every day.

Why is it famous?
It's new. It's a
symbol of Tokyo.

Big Ben

What is it?
It's a tower.

Where is it?
It's in London, UK.
It's next to the River
Thames.

When is it open?
It isn't open to
tourists.

Why is it famous?
It's old. It's a symbol
of London.

5 Pronunciation *th* /ð/

a ▶ 71 Listen and repeat the conversations from Exercise 4.

b Practise the *th* sound in these words.

this	that	these	those	there
they	the			

Reading

6 Read about *The Skytree* and *Big Ben*.
Choose the correct option.

1 *The Skytree / Big Ben* is in Europe.
2 *The Skytree / Big Ben* is open to tourists.
3 *The Skytree / Big Ben* is near a river.

Grammar question words

▶ QUESTION WORDS

What is it?	*When* is it open?
Where is it?	*Why* is it famous?

Now look at page 164.

7 Complete the questions with the correct question word.

1 Q: _____ are you?
  A: I'm in the park.
2 Q: _____ is the museum open?
  A: Every day.
3 Q: _____ is the name of this street?
  A: Oxford Street.
4 Q: _____ is this place famous?
  A: It's very old.
5 Q: _____ is this?
  A: It's in Italy.
6 Q: _____ is your holiday?
  A: In June.

Speaking ⟨ my life ⟩

8 Work in pairs. Ask and answer questions about two places.
Student A: Turn to page 153.
Student B: Turn to page 155.

4c Time zones

Vocabulary the time

1 ▶ 73 Match the times with the clocks. Listen, check and repeat.

a	`11:00`	eight twenty
b	`9:30`	eleven o'clock
c	`16:15`	three fifty-five
d	`19:45`	four fifteen
e	`20:20`	seven forty-five
f	`15:55`	nine thirty

2 Write *morning*, *afternoon* or *evening* for the times in Exercise 1.

3 ▶ 74 Listen and write the times.

1 ....   4 ....
2 ....   5 ....
3 ....   6 ....

4 Match the word with the time.

1 midday   24.00
2 midnight   12.00

5 Work in pairs. Ask and answer questions.

What time is	your the	English class? office open? school open? bus in the morning? train to work? café open?

Reading

6 Read *Time zones* and look at the map. Where is the International Date Line?

7 Read *Time zones* again. Look at the time in London. Write the names of the two cities.

London: 12.00
1 .... : 20.00
2 .... : 07.00

8 Work in pairs. It's midday in London. What time is it in these places?

Cairo   Rio de Janeiro   Sydney Los Angeles   Perth   Lima

In Cairo, it's two o'clock in the afternoon.

9 What time and day is it where you are now? What time and day is it in London now?

10 Word focus *at*

a Underline three expressions with *at* in *Time zones* on page 51.

b ▶ 75 Complete the exchanges with these expressions. Listen and check.

at five o'clock   at home   at school at work

1 A: Where are your children? Are they here?
  B: No. It's two o'clock – they're
     ....

2 A: Sandy, what time is your train?
  B: It's ....

3 A: Hi, Tom. Are you .... ?
  B: No, I'm not. It's a holiday today. I'm
     ....

Speaking ⟨ my life ⟩

11 Work in pairs. Ask about different days and times. Take turns.

at home	in a car
at school	in bed
at work	in the city
in a café	in the classroom

It's Tuesday. It's nine thirty in the evening. Where are you?

I'm at home.

TIME ZONES ▶ 76

In **London**, it's twelve o'clock midday. Shops and offices are open. People are at work. Children are at school. In **Hong Kong**, it's eight o'clock in the evening. Schools are closed and children are at home. People are in cafés and restaurants. In **Los Angeles**, it's four o'clock in the morning. People aren't at work. They're at home. They're in bed.

The time is different in the 24 time zones in the world. **Lima** and **New York** are in the same time zone. Hong Kong and **Perth** are in the same time zone. **Sydney** and Perth are in different time zones. The International Date Line is the end of one day and the beginning of the next day. It's 80 kilometres from **Russia** to **Alaska**, but Sunday in Russia is Saturday in Alaska.

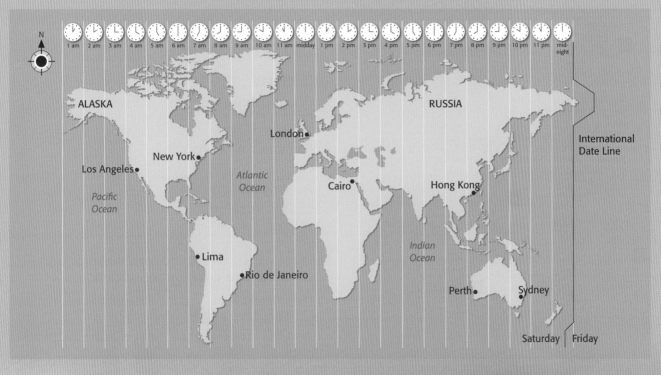

4d Two teas, please

Vocabulary snacks

1 ▶ **77** Write the words with the photos (a–j). Listen, check and repeat.

> apple   banana   cake   coffee
> fruit juice   mineral water   orange
> salad   sandwich   tea

mineral water

Real life buying snacks

2 ▶ **78** Listen to three conversations. Number the snacks (1–3) in Exercise 1.

3 ▶ **78** Complete the conversations with expressions for BUYING SNACKS. Listen again and check.

1   A: Hi. Can I help you?
    C: ¹ _____
    A: ² _____
    C: Small.
    A: Anything else?
    C: ³ _____

2   A: Hi. Can I help you?
    C: ⁴ _____
    A: Anything else?
    C: Yes. A salad.
    A: OK. ⁵ _____

3   A: ⁶ _____
    C: A tea and a fruit juice, please.
    A: ⁷ _____
    C: Yes. Two cakes, please.
    A: OK. Here you are. Seven pounds, please.
    C: ⁸ _____

> **▶ BUYING SNACKS**
>
> | | |
> |---|---|
> | Can I help you? | Anything else? |
> | Two coffees, please. | No, thanks. |
> | Can I have a mineral | Four euros, please. |
> | water, please? | Here you are. |
> | Large or small? | |

4 Pronunciation linking with *can*

a ▶ **79** Listen and repeat these sentences.

1   Can‿I help you?
2   Can‿I have a mineral water, please?

b Work in pairs. Practise the conversations in Exercise 3.

5 Work in pairs. Take turns to buy a snack from your partner.

> *Hi. Can I help you?*

> *Two teas, please.*

4e See you soon

Writing a text message

1 Read the text message. Answer the questions.

1 Who is the text message to?
2 Who is it from? Where is she?

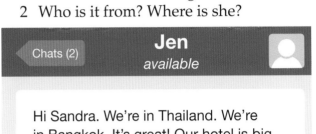

> **Chats (2)**
>
> **Jen**
> *available*
>
> Hi Sandra. We're in Thailand. We're in Bangkok. It's great! Our hotel is big and new. It's near the market in our photo. The markets are famous here. Thai people are friendly and Thai food is great.
>
> See you soon.
>
> *11.55*

2 Read the text message again. Underline:

1 one adjective to describe Bangkok
2 two adjectives to describe the hotel
3 one adjective to describe the markets
4 one adjective to describe the people
5 one adjective to describe the food

3 Writing skill *and*

a Read the text message again. Underline *and* in two sentences.

b Read the pairs of sentences. Write one new sentence.

1 The hotel is small. The hotel is new.
   *The hotel is small **and** new.*
2 The museums are big. The museums are old.
3 The park is open on Saturday. The park is open on Sunday.
4 The town is old. The town is beautiful.
5 It's famous in America. It's famous in Europe.
6 It's a town with a bus station. It's a town with a train station.

c Read the pairs of sentences. Write one new sentence.

1 Thai people are friendly. Thai food is great.
   *Thai people are friendly **and** Thai food is great.*
2 Our hotel is modern. The room is clean.
3 The beaches are great. The buildings are beautiful.
4 The airport is small. The plane is old.
5 The park is next to our hotel. The market is in our street.
6 London is big. Some parts are dirty.

4 Choose a place you know. Write a text message to your partner. Write about three of these things. Use *and*.

- the town/city
- places in the town/city
- the food
- the hotel
- the people

5 Check your text message. Check the adjectives and your spelling.

6 Exchange text messages with your partner. Where is your partner?

4f Where's that?

WIPEOUT TO GO

SNACKS

Chicken Quesadilla	$6.50
Chicken Tenders with Fries	$5.95
Chili in a Bread Bowl	$6.25
Cheese Nachos	$5.50
Onion Rings	$3.95
Chili Cheese Fries	$4.95
Garlic Fries	$4.95
French	$2.95 / $3.95

SEA FOOD

Crispy Fried Calamari & Chips	$6.50
Coconut Shrimp & Chips	$6.95
Popcorn Shrimp & Chips	$6.95
Jumbo Shrimp Cocktail	$5.95
Mango Glazed Pork Ribs	$6.95
Fish & Chips	$6.95

BURGERS

Served with lettuce, tomato & onion.
Combo Meal – add fries and small soda $2.50

Hamburger	$5.50
Cheeseburger	$5.95
BBQ Burger	$6.25
Fried Fish Sandwich	$6.25
BBQ Pork Sandwich	$6.95

PIZZAS
(By the Slice)
Made in our pizza oven with fresh mozzarella cheese

Cheese	$4.25	Pepperoni	$4.95
BBQ Chicken	$4.95	Vegetarian	$4.50

TACOS (1 / $3.75   2 / $6.75   3 / $9.50)
Made with corn tortillas, cabbage, jalapeño-lime cream

Fish Tacos – grilled with sautéed onions & peppers
Grilled Chicken – sautéed onions & peppers
Grilled Steak – sautéed onions & peppers

DRINKS

Sodas small-$2.25 large-$2.75
Coke, Diet Coke, Root Beer,
Sprite and Lemonade

Bottled Water small-$2.00

Sales tax will be added to all menu items

EAT. DRINK. SURF.

PICK-UP

ORDER HERE

EAT
DRINK
SURF

TAKE OUT

A snack bar near the beach

Before you watch

1 Look at the photo and the caption on page 54. Find the name for this place in the word box.

2 Key vocabulary

a Read the sentences (1–3). Match the underlined words with a–c .

1 Oxford Street is a big <u>shopping street</u> in London.
2 The name of the café is on the <u>sign</u>.
3 Tower <u>Bridge</u> is in London. It's on the River Thames.

b ▶ 80 Listen and repeat the <u>underlined words</u>.

3 ▶ 81 Look at the word box. Listen and repeat the words.

4 Work in pairs. Are these places in your town? Where?

> a bridge   a garden   a shopping street
> a snack bar

5 Work in pairs. Tick (✓) the things in your city or town.

> | | |
> |---|---|
> | a bank | a market |
> | a bus station | a museum |
> | a café | a park |
> | a car park | an information centre |
> | a cinema | a train station |

While you watch

6 🎦 4 Watch the video. Are the things in your list from Exercise 5 in the video?

7 🎦 4 Watch the video again. Where are the cities? Write the number of the city (1–4) with the continent. Two cities are in one continent.

> America   Asia   Europe

8 Work in pairs. What are the names of the four cities? Choose the correct option (a–c). Do you agree with your partner?

1 a Beijing   b Hong Kong c Tokyo
2 a Madrid   b Paris   c Rome
3 a New York b San Francisco
   c Washington
4 a Lisbon   b London
   c St Petersburg

After you watch

9 Look at the questions and answers from the video. Complete the questions.

A: That's beautiful. ¹_____'s that?
B: It's in the city. It's a park with a lake.
A: ²_____'s that? Is that you next to the lake?
B: No, it isn't.
A: ³_____'s that? A park?
B: It's a garden – and a nice café next to the garden.
A: Look at the two people. ⁴_____ are they there?
B: I don't know.
A: ⁵_____ are the people?
B: They're tourists, I think.

10 Match two places with each city from the video. Then write sentences about one of the cities.

> Atocha Station
> Fisherman's Wharf
> Greenwich Naval College
> Shinjuku district
> the Golden Gate bridge
> the Imperial Palace
> the London Eye and the Houses of
>   Parliament
> the Prado museum

 a garden
(noun)
/'gɑːdən/

 a snack bar
(noun)
/'snæk ˌbɑː/

 lights
(noun)
/laɪts/

 surf
(verb)
/sɜːf/

Grammar

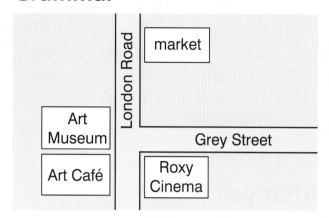

1 Look at the map. Complete the text about the Art Café.

The Art Café is a new café. It's ¹ .... London Road. It's ² .... the Art Museum. It's open Monday – Saturday, from 10.00 to 18.00 and from 10.00 to 14.30 on Sunday. It's ³ .... the Roxy Cinema and it's ⁴ .... London Road market.

2 Complete the questions about the Art Café.

1 .... is the café?
2 .... is it open?
3 .... is next to the Art Café?

3 ≫ MB Work in pairs. Ask and answer the questions from Exercise 2.

4 Choose the correct option.

1 Is *these / this* the bus to Oxford?
2 Are *that / those* apples?
3 Is *that / those* the train station?
4 *These / That* are my photos.

I CAN	
describe the location of places (prepositions of place)	☐
use *this*, *that*, *these* and *those* correctly	☐
ask and answer questions (question words)	☐

Vocabulary

5 Complete the words for places in a town.

1 b _ n k
2 c _ r p _ r k
3 _ n f _ rm _ t _ _ n c _ ntr _
4 tr _ _ n st _ t _ _ n

6 ≫ MB Work in pairs. Where are the places in Exercise 5 in your town?

7 ≫ MB Work in pairs. Take turns.
Student A: Choose a clock. Say the time.
Student B: Point to the clock.

8 Complete the menu with these words.

salad   fruit juice   coffee   sandwiches

The Art Café		
Cold drinks		
mineral water		€1.00
2		€1.50
Snacks		
3		€2.00
4		€2.00
cake		€1.50
Hot drinks		
tea		€1.00
1		€1.50

I CAN	
talk about places in a town	☐
say the time	☐
talk about snacks	☐

Real life

9 Complete the conversation in a café with a–e.

a Anything else?
b OK. Eight euros, please.
c Large or small?
d Thanks.
e Hello. Can I help you?

A: ¹ ....
B: Can I have two teas, please?
A: ² ....
B: Small, please.
A: ³ ....
B: Yes. Two sandwiches.
A: ⁴ ....
B: Here you are.
A: ⁵ ....

10 Practise the conversation in Exercise 9. Change the snacks.

I CAN	
buy snacks	☐

Unit 5 My things

The 'jetman' in the air

FEATURES

1 Look at the photo and the caption. Where is the 'jetman'?

2 ▶ 82 Read the sentences. Then listen and write true (T) or false (F).

1 Yves Rossy is from Switzerland.
2 He can fly.
3 He's in the air for nine minutes.

3 ▶ 82 Listen again. Why is the photo fantastic?

4 Work in pairs. <u>Underline</u> two things that can fly.

birds   fish   lions   planes

5a Robots and people

ROBOTS AND PEOPLE

▶ 83

The woman on the left is 69-year-old Nabeshima Akiko. She's in a supermarket in Japan. She's with a robot. The robot is from Keihanna Science City near Kyoto. This robot can see and it can speak. It can move, but it can't run. It can carry things – for example, Nabeshima's basket.

Robots are amazing. They can help people in their lives.

Reading

1 Look at the photo. Find:

two women	a robot	a child	a basket

2 Read the article. <u>Underline</u>:

1 the woman's name
2 four things this robot can do
3 one thing this robot can't do

Grammar *can/can't*

▶ **CAN/CAN'T**

I/You		
He/She/It	can	see.
We/You/They	can't	run.

(can't = cannot)

Now look at page 166.

3 Choose the correct option to make a true sentence.

Robots *can / can't* help people.

4 Write sentences with *can* and *can't*.

1 robots / move ✓
  Robots can move.
2 robots / speak ✓
3 robots / carry things ✓
4 people / fly ✗
5 I / speak English ✓
6 my grandfather / run ✗

5 Pronunciation *can/can't*

▶ **84** Listen and check your sentences from Exercise 4. Listen again and repeat.

Vocabulary abilities

6 ▶ 85 Listen. Tick (✓) the sentences that are true for you. Make the other sentences negative.

1 I can cook.

2 I can speak English.

3 I can play table tennis.

4 I can drive a car.

5 I can ride a bike.

6 I can swim.

7 I can sing.

8 I can play the piano.

7 Work in pairs. Take turns.
Student A: Read your sentences to your partner.
Student B: Write the number of the sentence. Then write (*can*) or (*can't*).

Listening

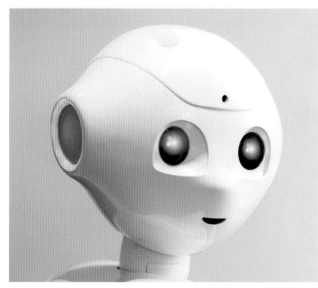

8 ▶ 86 Listen to an interview about a robot called Tomo. Are the sentences true (T) or false (F)?

1 The robot's name is Tomo.
2 Tomo is an American robot.
3 Tomo is a new kind of robot.
4 'Tomo' is Japanese for 'intelligent'.

9 ▶ 86 Listen again. What are the answers to the questions? Write ✓ (*can*) or ✗ (*can't*).

1 Can Tomo speak Japanese?
2 Can she sing?
3 Can she play the piano?
4 Can she swim?

Grammar *can* questions and short answers

▶ CAN QUESTIONS and SHORT ANSWERS		
Can	I/you he/she/it we/you/they	speak Japanese? swim?
Yes, No,	I/you he/she/it we/you/they	can. can't.

Now look at page 166.

10 Look at the grammar box. Write short answers to the questions in Exercise 9.

Speaking ⟨ my life ⟩

11 Work in pairs. Ask and answer questions about the abilities in Exercise 6.

Can you cook?

Yes, I can. / No, I can't.

5b Our things

Vocabulary possessions

1 Look at the photos. Write the words with the photos.

a camera	a cat	a football	glasses
a guitar	a motorbike	photos	a watch

2 ▶ 87 Listen and check your answers from Exercise 1. Repeat the words.

3 Work in pairs. Test your memory. Take turns.

What's 'b'?

A football?

Yes.

Our THINGS

Every family in the United Kingdom has at least one of these things. What about you?

Listening

4 ▶ 88 Listen to four people. Write their possessions.

person 1 _____

person 2 _____

person 3 _____

person 4 _____

5 ▶ 88 Listen again. Complete the descriptions.

1 It has a _____ on it – 1921. It's very _____ .

2 He has _____ coloured eyes. One is _____ and one is _____ .

3 The astronauts at NASA have the same glasses. They're very _____ .

4 It's from a game between Portugal and _____ . It has _____ 's signature on it.

6 Work in pairs. Why are the possessions interesting?

Grammar *have/has*

▶ **HAVE/HAS**

I/You/We/You/They	*have*	a motorbike.
He/She/It	*has*	glasses.

Now look at page 166.

7 Look at the grammar box. Look at the sentences. Choose the correct option.

1 My football *have / has* a signature on it.
2 My friends *have / has* a piano.

8 Complete the sentences with *has* or *have*.

1 I _____ a bike. It's new.
2 My friend _____ a motorbike. It's old.
3 My brother _____ two cameras. They're expensive.
4 My sister _____ a bag. It's black.
5 My friends _____ a car. It's small.
6 I _____ two sisters. They _____ brown eyes.

9 Pronunciation *have/has*

a ▶ 89 Listen and check your sentences from Exercise 8. Listen again and repeat.

b Work in pairs. Tell your partner about two of your possessions.

> *I have a camera. It isn't new. It's a Nikon.*

Grammar *be* + adjective

▶ **BE + ADJECTIVE**

*My cat is **beautiful**.*
*Your children are **young**.*
*His camera isn't **expensive**.*
*Are these glasses **new**?*

Now look at page 166.

10 Look at the grammar box. Are adjectives the same with singular and plural nouns? Or are they different?

11 Write the words in order. Make sentences and questions.

1 car / our / new / isn't
2 old / is / camera / your / ?
3 beautiful / children / our / are
4 interesting / are / her / photos / very
5 bag / black and white / his / is / ?
6 is / very / piano / old / their

Speaking ⌐my life⌐

12 Work in pairs. Talk about three of your possessions, animals or family members.

> *I have two brothers. Juan's eyes are blue and Antonio's eyes are brown.*

5c Technology and me

Vocabulary technology

1 Look at the objects. Number the words (1–7).

a battery	a webcam
a camera	apps
a memory stick	headphones
a screen	

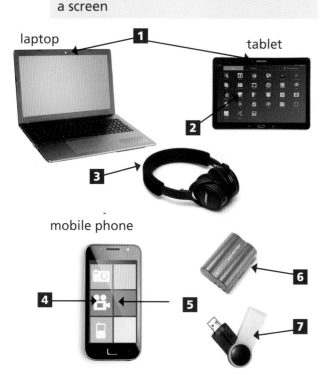

laptop

tablet

mobile phone

2 Work in pairs. Can you do these things with a mobile phone? And with a laptop or a tablet?

1 talk to people
2 take photos
3 take videos
4 play music
5 listen to music
6 send emails

Reading

3 Read the *Intelligent travel blog*. Who is the blog about?

4 Read the blog again. Find these adjectives. What do they describe?

small	new	big	expensive	good
old	nice	great		

Grammar adjective + noun

> ► **ADJECTIVE + NOUN**
>
> 1a This **camera** is **old**.
> 1b It's an **old camera**.
> 2a These **headphones** are **great**.
> 2b They're **great headphones**.
>
> Now look at page 166.

5 Look at the words in bold in the grammar box. Circle the adjectives and underline the nouns.

6 Look at the second sentence in each pair (b). Is the adjective before or after the noun?

7 Write the adjective in the correct place in the sentence.

1 It's a laptop. *fantastic*
   It's a fantastic laptop.
2 These are batteries. *new*
3 They're headphones. *expensive*
4 This is an app. *great*
5 I have a phone. *old*
6 My phone has a memory. *big*

8 Read the pairs of sentences. Write one new sentence.

1 I have a bag. It's nice.
   I have a nice bag.
2 That's a laptop. It's fantastic.
3 Jack has a passport. It's new.
4 I have two televisions. They're black.
5 We have a map of the world. It's old.
6 These are my sunglasses. They're expensive.

Speaking ⌐my life⌐

9 Work in pairs. Talk about your favourite piece of technology. Are your favourite pieces of technology the same – or different?

> What's your favourite piece of technology?

> My tablet.

> Why?

> It's small and it has a great screen.

INTELLIGENT TRAVEL **blog**

▶ 90

This week we ask a newspaper reporter about the technology in her travel bag. Here are her answers.

What's in your travel bag?

This is my 'mobile office'. These things are in my bag. I have them with me on every trip. It isn't a small bag!

Which things are expensive?

Well, I have a new camera. It has a big memory. It can take hundreds of photos. And my laptop is expensive too. It has a good battery – I can work on planes and trains with no problems.

What about your phone?

I have an old phone, but it's very good. It has a nice camera. I can see and talk to my family at home.

What about music?

My phone has a good app for music and I have great headphones. I can listen to music all the time.

my life   ▶ MY ABILITIES   ▶ MY THINGS   ▶ **MY FAVOURITE PIECE OF TECHNOLOGY**   ▶ SHOPPING
▶ AN EMAIL

5d How much is it?

Vocabulary money and prices

1 Work in pairs. Match these countries with their money (euros [€], pounds [£], dollars [$]).

Australia   Belgium   Canada
Germany   Ireland   New Zealand
the United Kingdom   the United States

2 ▶ 91 Listen and repeat the prices.

a £2.30
b £13.50
c €15.00
d €3.75
e $17.80
f $18.00

3 Pronunciation numbers

a ▶ 92 Listen and tick (✓) the correct price.

1 £13.00   £30.00   4 £16.00   £60.00
2 £14.00   £40.00   5 £17.00   £70.00
3 £15.00   £50.00   6 £18.00   £80.00

b ▶ 92 Listen again and repeat the prices.

c Work in pairs. Take turns to dictate three prices to your partner.

Real life shopping

4 ▶ 93 Listen to three conversations. Write the number of the conversation (1–3) next to the product. There is one extra product.

an alarm clock   books

sunglasses   memory sticks

5 ▶ 93 Listen to the conversations again. Tick (✓) the correct price.

1 €15   €50   €80
2 £46.50   £65.60   £95.50
3 £5.99   £9.99   £99

6 Look at the expressions for SHOPPING. Write customer (C) or shop assistant (A).

> **▶ SHOPPING**
>
> Excuse me.
> Can I help you?
> I'd like these sunglasses, please.
> How much is this alarm clock?
> How much are these memory sticks?
> It's / They're €50.
> That's £95.50, please
> Can I pay with euros / cash / a credit card?
> Here you are.

7 Work in pairs. Look at the audioscript on page 185. Practise the conversations.

8 Work in pairs. Take turns to buy a product.
Shop assistant: Decide the price.
Customer: Decide how much you can pay.

a wallet   a purse

a tablet   pens

my life   ▶ MY ABILITIES   ▶ MY THINGS   ▶ MY FAVOURITE PIECE OF TECHNOLOGY   ▶ SHOPPING
▶ AN EMAIL

5e Can you help me?

Writing an email

1 Read the email. Answer the questions.

  1 Who is the email from?
  2 Who is the email to?

2 Read the reply. Complete the table.

	Positive +	Negative -
Tablets	can write on the screen	screens
Laptops	have a touchscreen have a keyboard fast	

Computer Life *Weekly*

can help with your IT questions.

Email mike@computerlifeweekly.com

Hi Mike

I'm a student at college. I'd like a new computer. My PC is old and slow. I can buy a laptop or a tablet. I can't decide. Can you help me?

Eliza

Hi Eliza

Tablets have good screens, but they're small. You can write on the screen. That's great. Laptops can have a touchscreen or a keyboard. Good laptops are fast, but they're expensive. I hope this helps.

Good luck in your studies!

Mike, Computer Life Weekly

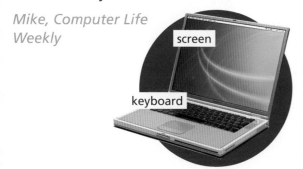

screen

keyboard

3 Writing skill *but*

a Underline two sentences with *but* in Mike's reply.

b Read the pairs of sentences. Write one new sentence with *but*. Add a comma (,) before *but*.

  1 This tablet is great. It's expensive.
  2 The screen isn't big. It's nice.
  3 My car is old. It's fast.
  4 My PC isn't old. It's slow.
  5 Our doctor is young. She's good.
  6 The book is old. It's interesting.

c Complete the sentences with *and* or *but*. Add a comma (,) before *but*.

  1 The wallets are very expensive _____ they're nice.
  2 My grandfather is old _____ he's grey.
  3 Your car is old _____ it's fast.
  4 These cameras aren't digital _____ they're good.
  5 The cat is young _____ it's big.
  6 Learning English is easy _____ it's interesting.

4 Complete the email with seven of these words.

can	can't	a bike	a motorbike	bus
cheap	expensive	fast	slow	

I'm a student at college. The ¹_____ to college is ²_____ , but it's ³_____ . I can buy a ⁴_____ or a ⁵_____ . I ⁶_____ decide. ⁷_____ you help me?

5 Work in pairs. Compare your emails. Say one positive and one negative thing about a bike and a motorbike.

5f What's your favourite gadget?

an **appointment** (noun)
/əˈpɔɪntmənt/ a meeting at a fixed time

busy (adjective)
/ˈbɪzi/ 'I'm very busy today – I have six appointments!'

 an **engineer** (noun)
/endʒɪˈnɪə/

a **gadget** (noun)
/ˈɡædʒɪt/ a piece of technology

organize (verb)
/ˈɔːɡənaɪz/ to plan

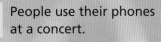

People use their phones at a concert.

Before you watch

1 Look at the photo on page 66. What gadgets can you see?

2 Key vocabulary

Read sentences 1–4. Match the underlined words with the pictures (a–d).

1 My <u>kitchen</u> is very small. I can cook in it, but I can't eat in it.
2 I can make great coffee in my new <u>coffee machine</u>.
3 I can cook lots of different food in my <u>microwave oven</u>.
4 My <u>office</u> is in the centre of town.

b ▶ 94 Listen and repeat the underlined words.

3 ▶ 95 Look at the word box on page 66. Listen and repeat the words.

4 Work in pairs. Tell your partner the gadgets you have and where they are.

a camera	a memory stick
a coffee machine	a microwave oven
a laptop	a mobile phone

I have a laptop in my office.

I have a microwave in my kitchen.

5 In the video, Ashley and Clare talk about their favourite gadgets. What do you think the gadgets are?

While you watch

6 📹 5 Watch the video and check your ideas from Exercise 5.

7 Work in pairs. What can you remember about the two gadgets?

8 📹 5 Watch the video again. Tick (✓) the options (a–c) you hear.

Ashley's favourite gadget … .
a has a diary   c has a camera
b is expensive

Clare's favourite gadget … .
a is basic   c can make coffee
b is Italian   in two minutes

9 📹 5 Can you remember who says these things? Write Ashley (A) or Clare (C). Then watch the video again and check.

1 _____ is very busy.
2 _____ has a new gadget.
3 _____ has a bad memory.
4 _____ has a lot of gadgets.
5 _____ can talk to the gadget.

After you watch

10 Complete the information about the gadgets with the words.

camera	email	friends	office
phone	photos	photos	

My phone has a great [1] _____ . I can take fantastic [2] _____ and I can send them to my [3] _____ or to the computer in my [4] _____ . The [5] _____ from this phone are really, really good! And I can talk to my [6] _____ ! I can say 'Send this photo to John.' Or 'Send an [7] _____ to my office'. Or 'Call home'.

basic	coffee	expensive	friends
kitchen	microwave	ten	

Some coffee machines are [1] _____ , but my new machine is a [2] _____ machine and it isn't expensive. It's in my [3] _____ next to my [4] _____ . I have a lot of gadgets in my kitchen. I can make a cup of [5] _____ in two minutes. And it's fantastic coffee. I have [6] _____ different types of coffee! So I can make different types of coffee for my [7] _____ .

11 What's your favourite gadget? Why? Tell the class.

Grammar

1 Work in pairs. Ask and answer questions about Lynn. Use *can*. Take turns.

1 drive a car ✓
2 ride a bike ✗
3 cook ✓
4 play the piano ✓
5 speak Arabic ✗
6 speak Russian ✓
7 write in Arabic ✗
8 write in French ✗

2 ▶▶ MB Work in pairs. Make true sentences about yourself with the abilities in Exercise 1.

3 Complete the sentences with *have* or *has*.

1 I _____ brown eyes.
2 My brother _____ red hair.
3 My husband and I _____ a car.
4 Our friends _____ a nice house.
5 My friend _____ glasses.
6 My dad _____ a new camera.

4 ▶▶ MB Work in pairs. Make true or false sentences with *I have* + noun and these adjectives. Say *true* or *false* to your partner.

> beautiful   expensive   fantastic   great
> interesting   new   nice   old
> black, blue, etc.

I have a new car.

False.

> **I CAN**
> talk about ability (*can*)
> talk about possessions and features (*have*)
> describe objects (adjective + noun)

Vocabulary

5 Write ✓ or ✗ next to the objects.

1 You can take photos with:
   a camera   a cat   a motorbike
2 You can play music with:
   football   a guitar   photos
3 You can see with:
   glasses   photos   a watch
4 You can listen to music with:
   a battery   headphones   a screen

6 ▶▶ MB Work in pairs. Take turns.
Student A: Choose a price tag and say the price.
Student B: Point to the price tag.

$14.99   €50   £71.40   £13.30

€17.50 $19.90   €90.95   £45.70

> **I CAN**
> talk about abilities
> talk about possessions
> talk about technology
> talk about money

Real life

7 Complete the conversation between a customer (C) and a shop assistant (A) with these words. There is one extra word.

> are   help   here   like   much   pay
> that's   they're

A: Can I ¹ _____ you?
C: Yes. How ² _____ are these glasses?
A: ³ _____ €65. And those ones are €89.
C: OK. I'd ⁴ _____ these ones, please.
A: ⁵ _____ you are. ⁶ _____ €65.
C: Can I ⁷ _____ with a card?
A: Yes, of course.

8 Work in pairs. Practise the conversation in Exercise 8. Change the object and the price.

> **I CAN**
> buy snacks

Unit 6 We love it!

Sports fans in
Soweto, South Africa

70 My sport

The triathlon

72 My favourite things

A profile of a scientist
and a TV presenter

74 We love street food

Street food in the
Philippines

78 At the market

A video about people at
the market

1 Look at the photo. What's the sport?

2 ▶ 96 Look at these numbers. Listen and choose the correct option in sentences 1–3. Say the numbers.

100 = one hundred	1,000,000 = one million
1,000 = one thousand	

1 About 270 *thousand / million* people in the world play football.
2 Football is popular in about two *hundred / thousand* countries.
3 The World Cup prize is 30 *thousand / million* dollars.

3 Work in pairs. Take turns to say the numbers.

13,000,000	300	6,000,000	800
20,000	45,000	70,000,000	9,000

4 Work in groups. Answer the questions.

1 Which sports are popular in your country?
2 What sports can you play?

6a My sport

Vocabulary sports

1 Work in pairs. Write the words with the photos (a– e).

> basketball   cycling   swimming
> running   tennis

2 ▶97 Write the words from Exercise 1. Listen and check.

1 *Running* is a sport in the Olympic Games.
2 _____ is a sport in water.
3 _____ is a sport with bikes.
4 _____ is a sport with a ball for two or four people.
5 _____ is a sport with a ball for two teams.

Reading

MY SPORT

▶ 98

Hi! My name's Laura Todbury. My sport is the triathlon – swimming, cycling and running in one day. It's swimming for about one kilometre, then cycling for forty kilometres, then running for ten kilometres. I like swimming and cycling, but I don't like running. It's very hard. My best time for the triathlon is three hours and five minutes. It's not bad, but it's not very good. The best Olympic time for women is one hour and fifty-six minutes.

3 Look at the photo and the caption. What's the sport?

4 Read about Laura. Answer the questions.

1 What are the three parts of the triathlon?
2 How long is each part of the triathlon?
3 What's Laura's best time?

Grammar *like*

▶ **LIKE**

I/You/We/You/They	**like** **don't like**	basketball. tennis.
(don't = do not)		

Now look at page 168.

5 Look at the grammar box. Read about Laura again and underline the sentence with *like* and *don't like*.

6 Write sentences with *like* (☺) or *don't like* (☹).

1 I / tennis. ☺
I like tennis.
2 I / swimming. ☺
3 I / football. ☹
4 My friends / sport. ☺
5 I / basketball. ☹
6 We / Formula 1. ☺

7 ▶ 99 Listen and check your sentences from Exercise 6. Listen and repeat.

8 Change the sentences in Exercise 6 so that they are true for you. Read the sentences to your partner.

I don't like tennis.

Listening

9 ▶ 100 Listen to a conversation about sport. Tick (✓) the questions you hear.

a Do you like sport?
b Do your friends like sport?
c What sports do you like?

10 ▶ 100 Listen to the conversation again. Underline the answers to the questions.

1 Q: Do you like sport?
 A: Yes, I do. *I love sport! / No, I don't.*
2 Q: What sports do you like?
 A: *I like swimming and running. / My favourite sports are tennis and football.*

Grammar *like* questions and short answers

▶ **LIKE QUESTIONS and SHORT ANSWERS**

Do	I/you/we/you/they	**like**	tennis?
Yes, No,	I/you/we/you/they	**do.** **don't.**	

Now look at page 168.

11 Look at the grammar box. What's the question form of *like*?

12 Look at the grammar box again. Complete these questions and short answers.

1 _____ you _____ swimming?
 Yes, _____ _____ .
2 _____ they _____ cycling?
 No, _____ _____ .

13 ▶ 101 Write questions with *like*. Listen and check. What are the answers?

1 people in your family / sport?
2 What sports / you / on TV?
3 you / basketball?
4 you / swimming or cycling?

14 Pronunciation *do you ... ?*

a ▶ 102 Listen and repeat two questions from the conversation in Exercise 9.

b Work in pairs. Ask and answer the questions in Exercise 13.

Speaking ⌐ my life

15 Write a list of three sports you like. Write three questions with *Do you like ... ?*

16 Work as a class. Ask and answer your questions. Write the names of the people who like the same sport as you.

Bruno, do you like tennis?

No, I don't.

Carla, do you like tennis?

Yes, I do. I love tennis!

6b My favourite things

Vocabulary interests

1 ▶ 103 Look at the example. Match the words in A with the words in B. Listen and check.

comedies – films

A

comedies	pop
detective stories	wildlife shows
fish	scuba diving

B

animals   books   films

music   sports   TV

2 Write your favourite TV show, book, film and sport.
TV show – The Voice

3 Work in pairs. Ask and answer questions about the things in Exercise 2.

Do you like TV?   *Yes, I do.*

What's your favourite TV show?   *The Voice.*

Reading

4 Read the article about Dr Hogan. Underline three interests from Exercise 1.

5 Read the article again. Write true (T) or false (F).

1 Dr Hogan has two jobs.
2 He's a fisherman.
3 He's from Botswana.
4 His favourite sport is tennis.

My favourite things: **Dr Hogan**

▶ 104

```
Name: Dr Z Hogan
Place of Birth: Arizona
Current City: Reno, Nevada
Job: Professor, University
of Nevada and TV presenter:
Monster Fish, National
Geographic Television
```

Grammar *he/she + like*

► HE/SHE + LIKE

He/She		likes doesn't like	fish. cold places.
Does	he/she	like	coffee?
Yes, No,	he/she	does. doesn't.	

(doesn't = does not)

Now look at page 168.

6 What is the negative form of *likes*?

7 Write questions about Dr Hogan.

1 like / fish?
  Does Dr Hogan like fish?
2 like / Botswana?
3 like / Arizona?
4 like / cold places?
5 like / hot places?
6 like / coffee?

8 Work in pairs. Ask and answer the questions in Exercise 7 with short answers or *I don't know.*

Dr Hogan likes fish. He loves very big fish. He isn't a fisherman. He's a scientist. His job is to study fish in different places around the world – for example, in the Okavango Delta in Botswana. That's Dr Hogan's favourite place. He's from a big city in Arizona. It's a very hot, dry place. He doesn't like cold places very much. Does he like wet places? Well, he likes water! He loves swimming and scuba diving in his free time. He also likes wildlife shows on TV and coffee!

9 Write five sentences about Dr Hogan. Use *likes / doesn't like.*
  He likes fish.

10 Pronunciation *likes, doesn't like*

a ▶ 105 Listen to five sentences about Dr Hogan.

b ▶ 105 Listen again and repeat the sentences.

Speaking *my life*

11 Work in pairs. Look at the table. Take turns.
  Student A: Choose a person.
  Student B: Ask *Does she like … ?* to discover the person's identity.

Does she like music?

No, she doesn't.

Does she like books?

Yes, she does.

Is it Teresa?

Yes!

		Barbara	Diana	Stella	Teresa
🐾		✓	✓	✗	✗
📖		✗	✗	✓	✓
🎞		✗	✓	✗	✓
🎵		✓	✗	✓	✗
👟		✗	✓	✗	✓
🖥		✓	✗	✓	✗

12 Choose four friends or family members. Then work in pairs. Ask questions. Use *Does he/she like … ?*

6c We love street food

Vocabulary food

1 Write the words with the photos.

> bread   cheese   eggs   fruit   meat
> potatoes   rice   vegetables

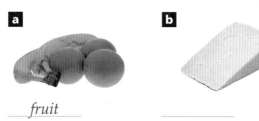

a *fruit*   **b** _____

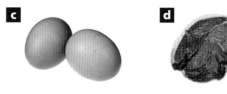

c _____   **d** _____

e _____   **f** _____

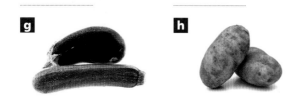

g _____   **h** _____

2 ▶ 106 Listen and check your answers from Exercise 1. Repeat the words.

3 Work in pairs. Talk about the food you like.

Reading

4 Read the article *We love street food*. Find three words that describe street food in the Philippines.

5 Read the article again. Find the food:

1 one person has for breakfast
2 one person has for lunch
3 one person has for dinner

6 Match the meals with the correct times.

Meals	Times
breakfast	morning
dinner	midday
lunch	evening

7 Work in pairs. What do you like for your meals? What do people in your country have for their meals?

Grammar object pronouns

▶ **OBJECT PRONOUNS**

Subject pronoun	Object pronoun
I	*me*
you	*you*
he	*him*
she	*her*
it	*it*
we	*us*
you	*you*
they	*them*

Now look at page 168.

8 Look at the grammar box. <u>Underline</u> two object pronouns from the box in *We love street food* on page 75. Rewrite the sentences with the nouns.

9 Choose the correct option.

1 I love vegetables. I have *it / them* every day.
2 The Philippines is a great country. I love *it / them*.
3 Can I help *me / you*?
4 Where's your sister? I can't see *her / you*.
5 This is my favourite café. I love *her / it*.
6 Your brother is nice. I like *her / him*.

Speaking ⟨ my life ⟩

10 Work in pairs. Turn to page 157.

We love street food

▶ 107

The Philippines has great restaurants, fantastic cafés and very good street food. You can buy lots of great food from stalls in the street. People in the Philippines love street food. Visitors to the Philippines love it too. It's easy, it's fun and it isn't expensive. What are people's favourite meals?

Aimee (Manila)
'I have *Lechon Manok* chicken for dinner every evening. I love it!'

Danilo (Tagaytay)
'I have *champorado* for breakfast. It's rice with chocolate, milk and sugar. I have it every day.'

Tala (Quezon City)
'Bananas are my favourite fruit. The food stall near my school has fantastic banana spring rolls. They're called *Turon*.'

Suzy (Los Angeles)
'Manila has great street food. My favourite snacks are rice cakes. I love them.'

Isko (Manila)
'I have breakfast at home, but I have street food for lunch. My favourite meal is *arroz calda*. It's soup with rice.'

 a **spring roll** (noun) /sprɪŋ 'rəʊl/

 a **stall** (noun) /stɔːl/

6d Let's play table tennis

Vocabulary opinion adjectives

1 ▶ 108 Look at the four opinion adjectives. Listen to three conversations. Match words from the conversations (1–3) with the four opinion adjectives.

1 sport
2 Felicity Jones
3 fish, pizza

boring

horrible

fantastic / great

2 Are the adjectives in Exercise 1 positive (+) or negative (-)? Write them in the table.

Positive +	Negative -

3 Pronunciation intonation

a ▶ 109 Listen and repeat the opinions.

b Make a list of four people or things. Give the list to your partner. Tell your partner your opinion of the things on their list.

Basketball's boring.

Real life suggestions

4 ▶ 108 Look at the expressions for making and responding to SUGGESTIONS. Listen again and write the numbers (1–3) with the expressions. Two expressions are in two conversations.

> ▶ **SUGGESTIONS**
>
> Let's watch football.
> Let's go to the cinema.
> How about pizza?
> That's a good idea.
> I love her.
> No, thanks.
> I'm sorry.
> I don't like sport very much.
> OK.

5 Add three ideas to the table below.

Let's	go to have invite play watch	a burger a film football my friends pasta tennis the cinema the park your brother	tonight. tomorrow. this weekend.
How about ...?			

6 Work in pairs. Take turns to make suggestions and respond with opinions.

7 Work in groups. Make suggestions and find an activity for this weekend.

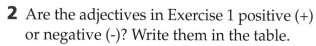

my life ▶ A SPORTS SURVEY ▶ A PUZZLE ▶ FOOD ▶ **SUGGESTIONS**
▶ SHORT MESSAGES

6e Can we meet on Sunday?

Writing short messages

1 Read the messages (1–4). What is each message about? Write the number of the message.

a a celebration ....
b a film ....
c a meal ....
d a sport ....

1 Can you come for lunch at 2 pm tomorrow?

2 Can we meet at the cinema at 8 pm? I have my English class from 6 to 7.30.

3 Can I invite my sister to your party?

4 Do you like Formula 1? I have two tickets for the race on Sunday.

2 Match the messages in Exercise 1 with the replies (a–d).

a Yes, I love it! Thanks!

b Yes, of course you can.

c Sorry, I can't. I'm at work until 3.30.

d That's no problem. 8 pm is great for me.

3 Writing skill punctuation and sentence structure

a Look at the messages and replies in Exercise 1 and 2. Find these punctuation marks.

capital letter	A B C D
full stop	.
comma	,
question mark	?
exclamation mark	!

b Read the sentences and add the correct punctuation.

1 we have tickets for the game tomorrow
2 yes I love their music
3 no my friend doesn't like animals very much
4 do you like matt damon's films
5 that TV show is boring
6 thanks for the book I love it

c Look at the messages and replies in Exercises 1 and 2 again. Circle the subject and underline the verb.

1 Can you come for lunch at 2 pm tomorrow?

d Write the words in order. Add the correct punctuation.

1 meet / we / tonight / can / ?
   Can we meet tonight?
2 like / chips / you / do / ?
3 film / this / great / is
4 like / your / does / pizza / friend / ?
5 very much / meat / like / I / don't
6 expensive / new / car / is / his / and

4 Write four different replies to the messages in Exercise 1. Check your word order and punctuation.

5 Work in pairs. Write a short message. Give it to your partner. Write a reply to your partner's message.

At the market

THE COVERED M
Fifty Quality Indepe

At the Covered Market in Oxford

Brie (noun)
/briː/

a **vegetarian** (noun)
/vedʒɪˈteərɪən/ a person
who doesn't eat meat

Before you watch

1 Look at the photos. Match the names with the photos.

   a a cheese stall

   b a fish stall

   c a fruit and vegetable stall

2 Key vocabulary

a Read the sentences. Match the <u>underlined</u> words (1–4) with the pictures (a–d).

   1 I don't like fish very much – I don't like the <u>bones</u>.

   2 I love French cheese. <u>Camembert</u> is my favourite.

   3 The <u>tomatoes</u> at this fruit and vegetable stall are great.

   4 I like bananas, but I don't like <u>peaches</u>.

a   **b**   **c**   **d**

b ▶ 110 Listen and repeat the <u>underlined words</u>.

3 ▶ 111 Look at the word box on page 78. Listen and repeat the words.

4 Work in pairs. Say things you can buy at a market. Take turns. How many things can you say in 30 seconds?

While you watch

5 📹 6 Watch the video and write the number (1–3) next to the question.

   a Which stalls do you like?

   b Is this your local market?

   c Tell us what you don't like.

6 Work in pairs. What can you remember? How many things in your list from Exercise 4 are in the video?

7 📹 6 Read the sentences. Then watch the video again and choose the correct option (a–c).

   1 Jan Szafranski likes the *cheese / fish / fruit and vegetable* stall.

   2 Amy Mills doesn't like *fruit / meat / vegetables*.

   3 Richard Lewis loves *English cheese / French cheese / tomatoes*.

8 📹 6 Watch the video again. Are the sentences true (T) or false (F)?

   1 Richard's school is near the market.

   2 Amy's favourite stall is the cheese stall.

   3 Jan can cook fish.

9 What can you remember? Who says these sentences? Write the name of the person.

   1 My house is in this street, so this is my local market

   2 Yes, this is my local market. And it's really great.

   3 My wife likes it, but I don't. It has bones. I don't like them.

   4 I can't think – maybe tomatoes. I don't like them very much.

   5 I'm a vegetarian.

After you watch

10 Work in pairs. Take turns to buy things.
Student A: You are in the market. Write your shopping list.
Student B: You have a stall in the market. Decide what you sell and the prices.

Grammar

1 Complete the article about Jenna with the correct from of *like*. Use affirmative, negative and question forms.

Jenna is a scuba diver. It's her job. She
¹ _____ it very much. But ² _____
cold water? ³ _____ boats? And what
are her interests? Read our interview with
Jenna and find out.

Jenna, you are a professional scuba diver. Why?

*Well, I ⁴ _____ swimming and scuba diving.
And I love the sea.*

⁵ _____ water?

*Yes and no. I ⁶ _____ cold water very much.
It isn't very nice.*

Is this your boat?

*Yes, it is. I have three boats. I ⁷ _____ big
boats. They're fantastic!*

And finally, what are your interests?

I ⁸ _____ sports. And I love action films too.

2 Replace the underlined words in the sentences with object pronouns.

1 Read the interview with <u>Jenna</u>.
2 Jenna loves <u>the sea</u>.
3 Jenna likes <u>big boats</u>.
4 Jenna doesn't like <u>cold water</u>.
5 Jenna likes <u>Liam Neeson</u>.

3 ≫ **MB** Work in pairs. Ask and answer questions about the things in 2–5 in Exercise 2.

I CAN	
talk about likes and dislikes (*like*)	
use object pronouns correctly	

Vocabulary

4 <u>Underline</u> the odd one out in each group.

1 chocolate   football   tennis
2 action films   comedies   pop music
3 films   meat   vegetables
4 cycling   scuba diving   wildlife shows
5 animals   basketball   fish
6 cheese   fruit   swimming

5 Choose the correct option.

1 I like Adele. She's *fantastic / horrible*.
2 I don't like vegetables. They're *great / horrible*.
3 I love running. It's *boring / great*.
4 I don't like action films. They're *boring / fantastic.'*

6 ≫ **MB** Work in pairs. Make true sentences with the adjectives in Exercise 5.

I CAN	
talk about sports	
talk about food	
talk about interests	
give positive and negative opinions (adjectives)	

Real life

7 Read the conversation. Choose the correct option.

A: Let's ¹ *have pasta / watch TV / play tennis* tonight.
B: That's a good idea. What's on?
A: A film with Eddie Redmayne.
B: Oh, ² *it's horrible / I don't like him / she's fantastic*.
A: How about an Emma Stone film? I have her new film on DVD.
B: ³ *No, thanks. / OK. Great. / Yes, it's great.* I like her a lot.

8 Work in pairs. Practise the conversation in Exercise 7 with the other two options.

I CAN	
give my opinion	
make and respond to suggestions	

Unit 7 Daily life

The festival of colours – the Holi festival – in Kolkata, India

FEATURES

1 Look at the photo and the caption. Answer the questions.

1 Where are the people? 2 What is the celebration?

2 ▶ 112 Work in pairs. Listen to information about the Holi festival. Choose the correct option.

1 The Holi festival is in *December / March.*
2 It's a celebration of *new life / family life.*
3 The festival is one or two *days / weeks.*

3 ▶ 113 The Holi festival is a celebration of spring. Look at these words for the four seasons. Listen and repeat the words.

spring   summer   autumn   winter

4 Work in pairs. Which months are the seasons in your country?

I'm from Peru. Winter is June, July and August.

7a Day and night

Vocabulary routines

1 Match the routines (1–7) with the
pictures (a–g).

1 I **get up** at *six o'clock* . *f*
2 I **have breakfast** at _____ .
3 I **start work** at _____ .
4 I **have lunch** in a _____ .
5 I **finish work** at _____ .
6 I **have dinner** at _____ .
7 I **go to bed** at _____ .

2 ▶ 114 Listen and complete the
sentences in Exercise 1 with times
and places.

3 Work in pairs. Write seven true or
false sentences about your routines.
Read the sentences to your partner.
Find your partner's false sentences.

I get up at five o'clock.

False!

No, it's true.

Reading

4 Look at the photo and the caption.
Where is it? What kind of class is it?

5 Read about one of the women in the
photo. Is her routine similar to your
routine?

▶ 115

DAY AND NIGHT

Chen Hong's day

My name's Chen Hong. I live
with my husband and his parents
in Shanghai. Every day, I get up
at 5.30. I go to an exercise class.
My husband and his parents
don't go to the class. After the
class, I have breakfast with my
friends. We like rice balls or
pancakes. I start work at 8.30. At
midday, I have lunch. I don't work in the afternoon. In
the evening, I make dinner for my family. We eat at eight
o'clock. Then we watch TV. I go to bed at 10.30.

A morning exercise class on the Bund (riverside) in Shanghai

Grammar present simple *I/you/we/you/they*

▶ **PRESENT SIMPLE** *I/you/we/you/they*

I/You/We/You/They	***eat*** *at eight o'clock.* ***don't work*** *in the afternoon.*

Now look at page 170.

6 Look at the grammar box. What is the negative form of the present simple? Circle the affirmative and underline the negative verbs in the text *Day and night.*

7 ▶ 116 Complete the text about Roberto with these verbs. Listen and check.

finish	get up	go	not / go	~~have~~	have
start	work				

A night in Chile

I'm Roberto. I'm married and I ¹ *have* two children. I ² _____ in an observatory in Chile. I ³ _____ work at nine o'clock at night. I ⁴ _____ work at 2.30 in the morning and I go home and go to bed. At eight o'clock, I ⁵ _____ and I ⁶ _____ breakfast with my wife and children. They ⁷ _____ to school at 8.30. They ⁸ _____ to school on Saturday and Sunday.

8 Write one affirmative and one negative sentence with the verb in brackets.

1 I (work) *at home / in a shop.*
   I work at home.
   I don't work in a shop.
2 I (go) to bed *at ten o'clock / at midnight.*
3 You (study) *English / Spanish.*
4 My friends (have) a class *at 7.30 / at 8.30.*
5 I (eat) *burgers / fish.*
6 People in my country (have) lunch *at midday / at two o'clock or three o'clock.*

Grammar **prepositions of time**

▶ **PREPOSITIONS OF TIME**

at eight o'clock   *in the morning*

on Tuesday/Tuesdays   *at night*

Now look at page 170.

9 Look at the expressions in the grammar box. Underline similar expressions of time in the texts *Day and night* and *A night in Chile* in Exercise 7.

10 Complete the sentences with the correct preposition.

1 They don't work *at* night.
2 I don't go to school _____ the afternoon.
3 We have classes _____ Mondays and Wednesdays.
4 They watch TV _____ the evening.
5 We finish lunch _____ two o'clock.
6 You work _____ Saturdays.

Speaking ⟨ my life ⟩

11 Work in pairs. Find three things you both do at the same time. You can use some of these verbs. Write sentences with *We*. Use prepositions of time.

eat	have	get up	go
start	study	finish	

I eat at midday.

I eat at 12.30.

We don't eat at the same time.

7b Join the club

Vocabulary hobbies

1 ▶ 117 Look at the words and pictures.
Listen and number the words.

> climbing cooking dancing
> painting reading shopping
> singing walking

2 ▶ 117 Listen again and repeat the
words.

3 Work in pairs. Can you add more
activities to the list in Exercise 1? Ask
and answer questions.

> *Do you like reading?*
>
> *Yes, I do.*
>
> *No, I don't.*

Listening

4 ▶ 118 Look at the photo and the caption on
page 85. Listen to four people talk about their
hobbies. Complete the table.

	What?	When?	Why?
Andy	dressing up	1 _____	It's exciting
Tina	2 _____	in my free time	3 _____
Naga	4 _____	in the evening	5 _____
Paul	6 _____ and listening to music	7 _____	8 _____

5 ▶ 119 Match the questions (1–4) with the
answers (a–d). Listen and check.

1 Do you dress up every week?
2 Do your friends sing?
3 Do you eat your cakes?
4 Do you paint pictures of people?

a No, they don't. They play the guitar and
   the piano.
b No, we don't. We dress up in January.
c Yes, I do. Chocolate cake is my favourite.
d Yes, we do.

Grammar present simple questions *I/you/we/you/they*

> ▶ **PRESENT SIMPLE QUESTIONS**
> ***I/you/we/you/they***
>
> | **Do** | *I/you/we/you/they* | ***listen** to music?* |
> |---|---|---|
> | Yes,
> No, | *I/you/we/you/they* | ***do.***
> ***don't.*** |
>
> Now look at page 170.

6 Look at the grammar box. Then look at
the questions in Exercise 5. <u>Underline</u> the
question forms.

Friends dress up for the
Up Helly Aa festival.

Vikings (noun, plural) /ˈvaɪkɪŋz/

7 Put the words in order to make questions. Then answer the questions with true answers.

1 do / you / every Saturday / dress up / ?
2 enjoy / you / doing exercise / do / ?
3 you and your friends / do / go walking / ?
4 do / of your friends / you /take photos / ?
5 your parents / listen to music / do / ?
6 your friends / play table tennis / in the evening / do / ?

8 ▶ 120 Write questions with the words. Listen and check.

1 shopping (you / enjoy)
2 newspapers (you / read)
3 dancing (your friends / go)
4 basketball (you and your friends / play)
5 climbing (you / go)
6 TV (you and your friends / watch)

9 Pronunciation intonation in questions

a ▶ 120 Listen again and repeat the questions from Exercise 8.

b Work in pairs. Ask and answer the questions from Exercise 8.

Speaking   my life

10 Work in pairs. Add four questions about hobbies to the list in Exercise 8. Then work as a class. Ask questions. Find one person for each activity.

> Do you enjoy shopping, Bruno?

> No, I don't.

> Do you enjoy shopping, Carlos?

> Yes, I do.

7c A year in British Columbia, Canada

Vocabulary weather

1 ▶ 121 Look at the pictures. Listen and repeat the words.

cloudy   rainy   snowy

sunny   windy

2 ▶ 122 Listen to people from four places. Write the number (1–4) next to the weather word.

3 ▶ 122 Listen again. Match the number of the speaker with the country and season.

	Country	Season
1	Australia	autumn
2	Canada	spring
3	the United Kingdom	summer
4	South Africa	winter

4 Work in pairs. Describe the weather for seasons in your country.

> *I'm from Vietnam.*
> *Summer is hot and rainy.*

Reading

5 Look at the photos on page 87 and find:

> flowers   ice   leaves   trees

6 Read about the seasons in British Columbia. Match the paragraphs with the photos (a-d).

7 Read the article again. Underline the things people do in each season.

8 Work in pairs. Do people do the things in the article in your country? Tell your partner.

> *We don't go skiing in winter.*

Grammar present simple *Wh-* questions

▶ PRESENT SIMPLE *WH-* QUESTIONS			
What			**do**?
Where		*I/you*	**go**?
Who	**do**	*we/you/they*	**go** with?
Why		*people*	**go** to the beach?
When			**eat**?

Now look at page 170.

9 Look at the grammar box. Then look at the article. Find three *Wh-* question words from the grammar box in the article.

10 Complete the questions with *what, where, who, why* and *when*.

1 _____ do you go in summer?
2 _____ do you do in autumn?
3 _____ do flowers open?
4 _____ do you go cycling with?
5 _____ do you like winter?

Speaking ⌐ my life

11 Work in pairs. What's your favourite season? Ask and answer questions. Use these ideas.
- Why / like … ?
- What / do?
- When / do … ?
- Where / go?
- Who / go with?

> *My favourite*
> *season is winter.*

> *Why do you*
> *like winter?*

> *I like cold weather.*
> *We go skiing.*

▶ 123

A YEAR IN BRITISH COLUMBIA, CANADA

SUMMER

Where do people go in summer?

Summer is a great time for holidays here. The weather is hot and sunny. People go to the beach. They cook and eat outside. I go to Vancouver Island with my family. We go swimming in lakes and rivers.

AUTUMN

What do people do in autumn?

In autumn, classes start. Children go to school. Students go to university. It's cloudy and rainy. Trees change colour from green to brown. I think it's a beautiful season.

WINTER

Where do people go in winter?

In winter, it's cold, rainy and snowy too. A lot of people stay at home. They watch TV, read books and cook winter food. Winter is my favourite season. I like winter sports. I go to Whistler. It's in the mountains. I go skiing and climbing.

SPRING

Why do people like spring?

In spring, it's cloudy and rainy, but it isn't cold. Flowers open, birds sing and trees are green. People go cycling and running. They meet friends and they go for walks.

7d What's the matter?

Summer holidays in the United Kingdom

Vocabulary problems

1 ▶ 124 Look at the pictures and listen to seven people. Write the number (1–7) next to the picture.

a bored

b cold

c hot

d hungry

e thirsty

f tired

g wet

2 ▶ 124 Listen and repeat the expressions from Exercise 1.

3 Work in pairs. How do you feel right now? Tell your partner.

I'm hungry!

Real life problems

4 Work in pairs. Look at the photo. Describe the weather. Describe the people.

5 ▶ 125 Listen to the conversation. Write the names (F = father, P = Paul, A = Anna).

1 _____ is thirsty.
2 _____ doesn't feel well.
3 _____ is cold and wet.
4 _____ is bored.

6 ▶ 125 Listen again. Complete the mother's suggestions.

1 Why don't you have _____ ?
2 Why don't you eat _____ ?
3 Why don't you go _____ ?

> ▶ **PROBLEMS**
>
> What's the matter?
> I'm hungry/thirsty/cold/tired/hot/wet/bored.
> It's cold/wet/hot.
> I don't feel well.
> I don't like swimming.
> I don't understand.
> Why don't you have a cup of tea?

7 Pronunciation sentence stress

a ▶ 126 Listen to three sentences. Is *don't* stressed or unstressed?

b ▶ 126 Listen again and repeat the sentences.

8 Work in pairs. Look at the vocabulary in Exercise 1 and the expressions for talking about PROBLEMS. Take turns to talk about problems and make suggestions.

7e Meet our club members

Writing a profile

1 Read Hans's profile. <u>Underline</u> the true information.
Hans is *a student / married / in a photography club.*

2 Writing skill paragraphs

a Read Hans's profile again. Write the number of the paragraph.

  a interests: ....
  b professional information: ....
  c family / friends: ....

b Read the profile information for Jenna. Number the paragraphs (a–c) in order (1–3).

  a I live with three friends. We live in the city centre.
  b I like sports, singing and photography. I go to a lot of sports events. I take photos of sports people.
  c I'm a student. I go to the City College. In the summer holidays, I work at PLT Engineering.

c Read the notes for Luther. Organize the notes into three paragraphs.

> a teacher   engineering
> my wife and children   City College
> animals   photos

3 Make notes about yourself for a profile. Are you in a club or an organization?

- professional information
- family / friends   • interests

4 Use your notes and write three paragraphs.

5 Check your profile. Check the paragraph order, spelling and punctuation.

6 Give your profile to your partner. Find two things you have in common.

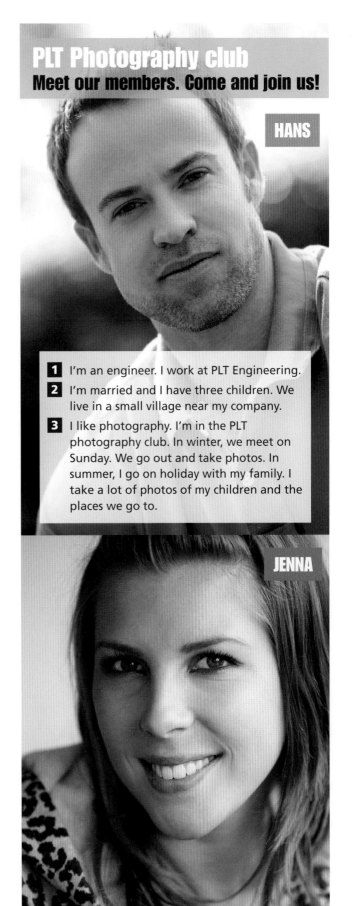

PLT Photography club
Meet our members. Come and join us!

HANS

1 I'm an engineer. I work at PLT Engineering.
2 I'm married and I have three children. We live in a small village near my company.
3 I like photography. I'm in the PLT photography club. In winter, we meet on Sunday. We go out and take photos. In summer, I go on holiday with my family. I take a lot of photos of my children and the places we go to.

JENNA

The elephants of Samburu

An elephant at night in Samburu National Reserve in Kenya

Before you watch

1 Work in pairs. Look at the photo and the caption. Where does this elephant live?

2 Key vocabulary

a Read the sentences. Match the underlined words with the pictures (a–f).

1 I sleep for eight hours every night.
2 My friend has a new jeep. It's fast.
3 I lie down after lunch on Sunday.
4 Put your hand up if you know the answer.
5 I have a bath in the morning.
6 The elephant has a long trunk.

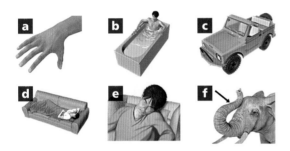

b ▶ 127 Listen and repeat the underlined words.

3 ▶ 128 Look at the word box. Listen and repeat the words.

4 Work in pairs. The video is about elephants in Kenya. Choose the option you think is correct.

1 Elephants live in *family groups* / *alone*.
2 Elephants *like* / *don't like* water.
3 Elephants eat *plants* / *animals*.
4 Elephants sleep *at night* / *in the afternoon*.

While you watch

5 ◻7 Watch the video. Check your answers from Exercise 4.

6 ◻7 Read the sentences. Watch the video again. Choose the correct option.

1 Nick Nichols is a *photographer* / *student*.
2 Daniel Lentipo *is a student* / *can identify individual elephants*.
3 Nick and Daniel follow the elephants for *four* / *ten* hours every day.
4 Elephants drink *alone* / *with other elephants*.
5 Elephants put their trunks up *to greet other elephants* / *when they are thirsty*.
6 Elephants *lie down* / *stand* to sleep.

7 ◻7 Watch the video again. Write:

1 six things the elephants do every day.
2 three things Nick and Daniel do every day.

After you watch

8 Complete the text with these verbs.

drive	follow	get up	start	take	walk
work					

Nick Nichols and Daniel Lentipo [1] .... at the Samburu National Reserve. They [2] .... early every day. They [3] .... work early. They [4] .... a jeep and [5] .... photos of the elephants. The elephants [6] .... many kilometres every day. Nick and Daniel sometimes [7] .... the elephants at night. Nick's photos of sleeping elephants are very unusual.

9 Work in pairs. Ask and answer questions using these ideas.

- What / favourite animals?
- Where / live?
- What / do?
- Why / like them?

---

call (verb) /kɔːl/ to make a noise (animal or bird)

 drink (verb) /drɪŋk/

follow (verb) /ˈfɑːləʊ/ to move behind a person or animal

gentle (adjective) /ˈdʒentl/ kind

greet (verb) /griːt/ to say 'hello'

identify (verb) /aɪˈdentɪfaɪ/ to find

an individual (noun) /ˌɪndɪˈvɪduəl/ one person or animal

 stand (verb) /stænd/

Grammar

1 Complete the text about two brothers with six of these words.

> brother cinema dinner food
> Friday music weekend

David and Yann are brothers. They have an internet company. From Monday to ¹_____ , they start work at seven o'clock. They finish work late and they have ²_____ in a restaurant. They like the same ³_____ . At the ⁴_____ , they don't do the same thing. David and his friends play ⁵_____ in a band. Yann and his girlfriend go walking and to the ⁶_____ .

2 Write the questions.

1 David and Yann / brothers?
2 they / work / in the same place?
3 where / they / have dinner?
4 they / like / the same food?
5 what / David and his friends / do / at the weekend?
6 Yann and his girlfriend / play music?

3 ≫ MB Work in pairs. Take turns.
Student A: Ask the questions in Exercise 2.
Student B: Cover the page. Answer the questions.

I CAN	
talk about personal information	
say what people do every day (present simple)	
say when people do things (prepositions of time)	

Vocabulary

4 Complete the adjectives. Write W (weather) and P (people).

1 b_r_d
2 cl__dy
3 h_ngry
4 sn__wy

5 s_nny
6 th_rsty
7 t_r_d
8 w_ndy

5 ≫ MB Work in pairs. Ask and answer the question with the adjectives from Exercise 4. Take turns.

> *What do you do when you're bored / it's snowy?*

> *I read a book.*

I CAN	
talk about daily routines	
talk about hobbies	
talk about the weather	
describe feelings (adjectives)	

Real life

6 Complete the sentences with the words. Then put the sentences in order to make a conversation.

> I'm No What's Why

a _____ don't you eat this pizza?
b _____ hungry.
c _____ thanks – it's cold.
d _____ the matter?

7 Work in pairs. Use these ideas to practise similar conversations. Take turns to start.

1 thirsty / cup of coffee
2 hot / drink of water
3 don't understand / use a dictionary
4 bored / go for a walk

I CAN	
talk about problems	
make suggestions	

Unit 8 Work and study

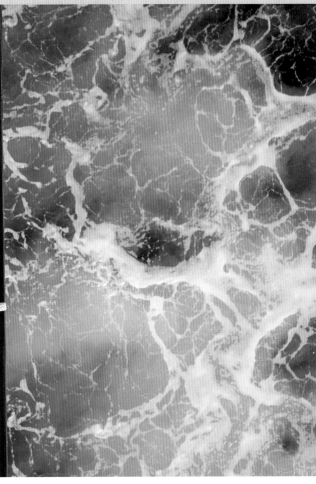

A man at work

1 Work in pairs. Look at the photo. Where is the man?

2 ▶ 129 Listen and choose the correct option.

1   This man's job is *in an office* / *outside*.
2   Every day is *different* / *the same*.
3   A painter's job *is* / *isn't* interesting.

3 Make true sentences about these jobs.

		inside.
Doctors		outside.
Engineers		in offices.
Painters		in cafés.
Photographers	work	in schools.
Teachers		in hospitals.
Waiters		with people.
		with children.

4 Work in pairs. Talk about the jobs in Exercise 3.

What do you do?

*I work with children.
I work in a hospital.*

You're a doctor.

8a It's a great job!

Reading

1 Work in pairs. Do you think these sentences are true (T) or false (F)? Look at the photo and the caption and check your ideas.

1 The London Underground has 270 stations.
2 The London Underground is also called the 'Tube'.
3 Parts of the London Underground aren't under the ground.

2 Read an article about two men, Naveen and Ryan. Find these things.

1 one job
2 one train line
3 one station

3 Read the article again. Answer the questions.

1 Do Naveen and Ryan like their jobs?
2 How many stations are on the Circle line?
3 Where do people buy tickets for the trains?

Grammar present simple *he/she/it*

▶ **PRESENT SIMPLE *HE/SHE/IT***

He/She/It	**opens** the train doors. **watches** the people. **doesn't work** at night.

Now look at page 172.

4 Look at the grammar box. <u>Underline</u> ten verbs with present simple forms in the article *It's a great job!*

5 Complete the sentences about Naveen and Ryan with the correct form of the verbs.

1 Naveen *enjoys* (enjoy) his job.
2 Naveen _____ (not / answer) people's questions.
3 Naveen _____ (not / work) at night.
4 Ryan _____ (help) people.
5 Ryan _____ (finish) work in the afternoon.
6 Ryan _____ (speak) to people in his job.

▶ 130

It's a great job!

Naveen and Ryan love their jobs. They both work on the 'Tube'.

Naveen is a train driver. He drives a train on the Circle line. The train stops at 36 stations. Naveen opens and closes the train doors. He watches the people.

Ryan works in the station at Baker Street. He doesn't drive a train. He checks people's tickets and he answers their questions. He doesn't sell tickets – people buy them from machines.

A busker in one of the London Underground's 270 stations. Only 45 per cent of the 'Tube' is under the ground.

6 ▶ **131** Complete the text about another London Underground worker with the present simple of the verbs. Listen and check.

| not / drive | ~~go~~ | help | look | walk |
| watch | work | | | |

Lily ¹ _goes_ to different Tube stations. She ² _____ a train. She's a police officer. Lily ³ _____ around stations. She ⁴ _____ people with problems. Sometimes, she ⁵ _____ in a big office. Lily ⁶ _____ the trains on computer screens and she ⁷ _____ at the cameras.

7 Pronunciation -s and -es verb endings

a ▶ **132** Listen and repeat the sentences with these verbs. Is the s like *this* or *is*?

| enjoys | goes | helps | works |

b ▶ **133** Listen to and look at the verbs. Underline the verbs with an extra syllable.

answer	answers
drive	drives
finish	finishes
look	looks
walk	walks
watch	watches

Vocabulary job activities

8 Look at these jobs. Complete the sentences with the jobs.

a doctor

a photographer

a receptionist

a shop assistant

a taxi driver

a waiter

1 A _____ answers questions.
2 A _____ drives people to different places.
3 A _____ takes photos.
4 A _____ sells things.
5 A _____ serves food and drink.
6 A _____ helps sick people.

Speaking and writing   my life

9 Choose a job. Work as a class. Ask questions about jobs. Find one name for each sentence. You have a time limit of five minutes.

Find a person in your class who ...
enjoys his or her job. _____
works in the mornings. _____
doesn't sell things. _____
talks to people. _____
doesn't work alone. _____
uses a computer. _____

> Do you enjoy your job, Bruno?

> No, I don't. It's boring.

> Do you enjoy your job, Che?

> Yes, I do. It's great!

10 Write six sentences about people in your class with the names.
Che enjoys her job.

8b At school

Vocabulary education

1 Look at the photo. Match seven of the words with things and people in the photo.

> board   book   classmate
> classroom   college   notebook
> pen   pencil   school   student
> teacher   university

2 Write four sentences with the words in Exercise 1. Work in pairs. Take turns to read your sentences to your partner – but don't say the word. Guess your partner's word.
The name of our school is London Languages.

> The name of our ... is London Languages.
>
> Yes.
>
> School?

Kakenya Ntaiya lives in Kenya. She has her own school. It's a school for girls. The girls live at the school. It's a primary school for year 4 to year 8.

Listening

3 Look at the photo and the information. Find Kakenya Ntaiya in the photo.

4 ▶ 134 Read these questions from a conversation about the school. Listen and put the questions in order (1–5).

a Does the school have many students?
b Does Kakenya work at the school?
c Does she teach?
d What does she do?
e Do the girls live at the school?   *1*

5 ▶ 134 Listen to the conversation again. Choose the correct answers to the questions.

1 *Yes, they do. / No, they don't.*
2 Yes, about *two / four* hundred.
3 *Yes, she does. / No, she doesn't.*
4 She's the *head teacher / president* of the school.
5 *Yes, she does. / No, she doesn't.*

6 Work in pairs. Do you think this school is unusual? Why? / Why not?

Grammar present simple questions *he/she/it*

▶ **PRESENT SIMPLE QUESTIONS *HE/SHE/IT***

		he/she	teach?
	Does	the school	**have** many students?
	Yes, No,	he/she/it	**does.** **doesn't.**
What Where	**does**	he/she	**do?** **live?**
		He/She	**'s** a teacher. **lives** in Kenya.

Now look at page 172.

7 Look at the grammar box. Complete these sentences to make questions.

1 _____ she _____ in Kenya?
   (live)
2 _____ he _____ in a shop?
   (work)

8 Write questions about Kakenya with these words.

1 study at the school?
   Does Kakenya study at the school?
2 work at the school?
3 work with girls?
4 what / do?
5 live in England?
6 where / live?

9 Work in pairs. Ask and answer the questions in Exercise 8.

1 *No, she doesn't.*

10 Complete the questions with *does* or *do*. Write true answers.

1 _____ boys study at Kakenya's school?
2 _____ your school have a café?
3 _____ your teacher live in England?
4 _____ your classmates live near you?
5 _____ your school open on Saturday?
6 _____ your English class start at 6 pm?

Speaking ⌐ my life ⌐

11 Work in pairs.
Student A: Turn to page 154.
Student B: Turn to page 156.

8c Helping big cats

Reading

1 Work in pairs. Match the animals in the photos (1–4) with the places (a–d).

a Africa and Asia   c South America
b Asia   d Africa

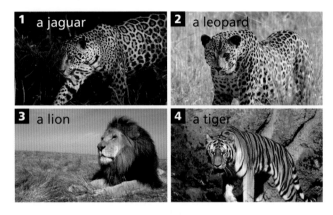

1 a jaguar
2 a leopard
3 a lion
4 a tiger

2 Work in pairs. Do you think the sentences are true (T) or false (F)?

1 Tigers are wild animals.
2 They eat animals.
3 They sleep at night.
4 Thailand has a lot of tigers.
5 Tigers live in forests.

3 Look at the photos and the captions, and read the article on page 99. Check your answers from Exercise 2.

4 Read the article again. Complete the sentences.

1 Tigers live in _____ .
2 Tigers kill _____ and
 _____ .
3 Saksit Simcharoen checks the
 _____ at night.
4 Saksit Simcharoen writes a _____ about the tigers in the park.

5 Answer the questions about the article.

1 How many wild tigers live in Asia?
2 How does Saksit study the tigers in the park?
3 How many tigers in the park have radio collars?
4 How often does Saksit write a report?

Grammar frequency adverbs

▶ FREQUENCY ADVERBS				
0%				100%
never	sometimes	usually	often	always
People	**sometimes**	move into forest areas.		
Tigers	**usually**	kill wild animals.		

Now look at page 172.

6 Look at the grammar box. What is the position of the frequency adverb in the sentences?

7 Rewrite the sentences with the adverb in the correct position.

1 People kill tigers. (sometimes)
2 Tigers live in forests. (often)
3 You see wild lions in South America. (never)
4 I watch nature shows on TV. (always)
5 My friends go to parks. (often)
6 I give money to animal organizations. (sometimes)

Speaking   my life

8 Make sentences 4–6 in Exercise 7 true for you. Tell your partner.

I often watch nature shows on TV.

9 Work in pairs. Ask follow-up questions to the sentences in Exercise 8.

What nature shows do you watch?

I watch a show called 'Earthpulse'.

Why don't you watch nature shows?

I don't enjoy them.

► 135

HELPING BIG CATS

'Big cats' is the name for tigers, lions, leopards and jaguars. The 'big cats' need our help.

A tiger in the forest at night in Sumatra, Indonesia

Tigers
number of wild tigers
in 1900 – 100,000;
in 2016 – 3,890

Tigers live in many places in Asia – from very cold mountains in the Himalayas to very hot areas. They usually live in places without people, but people sometimes move into forest areas with tigers. Tigers eat other animals. They usually kill wild animals, but they sometimes kill domestic animals. Tigers need our help because local people move into their areas and they sometimes kill the tigers.

Helping tigers
Tigers in Huai Kha
Khaeng Wildlife Park
in 1980 – 20;
in 2016 – 90

Saksit Simcharoen works at the Huai Kha Khaeng Wildlife Park in Thailand. The park is a very good place for tigers. Saksit goes into the forest at night. He doesn't see many tigers, but the park has 180 cameras. They can take a photo of a tiger. Saksit checks the cameras. About eight of the tigers in the park have radio collars. Every month, Saksit writes a report about the tigers in the area.

Saksit Simcharoen and his team in Thailand. They measure and put a radio collar on a tiger.

domestic (adjective) /dəˈmestɪk/ not wild, in homes and with people

a **radio collar** (noun) /ˌreɪdɪəʊ ˈkɒlə/

8d One moment, please

Real life on the phone

1 ▶ 136 Listen to three phone calls. Who does the caller want to speak to? Write the number of the conversation (1–3). Can the people answer the call?

a Mrs Jackson
b Ed Smith
c Mr Watts

2 ▶ 137 Look at the photos. Listen to two of the phone calls again. Why doesn't the caller speak to the person? Tick (✓) the reasons.

3 Look at the expressions for ON THE PHONE. Write caller (C) or receptionist (R).

> **▶ ON THE PHONE**
>
> Good morning. / Hello. PJ International.
> Can I help you?
> Yes, can I speak to Ed Smith, please?
> Yes, one moment, please.
> I'm sorry. He's / She's in a meeting.
> OK. Thank you. / Thanks.
> I'll call back later.

4 Complete the conversation with the expressions.

R: ¹ _____ . City College.
² _____ ?
C: Yes, ³ _____
   Mrs Jackson, please?
R: ⁴ _____ .
   She's out of the office at the moment.
C: OK. Thank you. ⁵ _____
   _____ . Goodbye.
R: Goodbye.

5 Pronunciation /s/ and /z/

a ▶ 138 Listen to these words. Is the <u>s</u> like thi<u>s</u> or i<u>s</u>?

> plea<u>s</u>e   he'<u>s</u>   ye<u>s</u>   Friday<u>s</u>   work<u>s</u>   thank<u>s</u>

b ▶ 138 Listen again and repeat the words.

works from home on Fridays

out of the office

on holiday

with a customer

doesn't work in the afternoons

in a meeting

6 Work in pairs. Practise phone calls. Use the ideas in the photos.

my life ▶ JOBS ▶ THINGS WE USUALLY DO ▶ ANIMALS ▶ ON THE PHONE ▶ AN EMAIL

8e My new job

Writing an email

1 Read Vijay's email about his new job in a call centre. Complete the email with seven of these words.

> classmates   colleagues   evening   job
> jobs   morning   office   phone calls   work

Hi!

Here I am in my new ¹ _____ ! It's good! I ² _____ from Monday to Friday. The ³ _____ opens at 8 am. I usually arrive at about 7.45 and I have coffee with my ⁴ _____ . They're great. We have a meeting every ⁵ _____ and the boss gives us our ⁶ _____ for the day. I usually make about forty ⁷ _____ every day. I finish early on Fridays – let's meet for lunch. How about next week?

Vijay

2 Read Vijay's email again. Who is it to?

a   his boss   c   his colleague
b   his friend

3 Writing skill spelling: double letters

a Read the email again. Underline the words with double letters.

b Complete the words with the letter. Add one letter or two. How many words have double letters?

1   ar_____ist (t)
2   busine_____man (s)
3   cla_____es (s)
4   co_____ege (l)
5   di_____erent (f)
6   di_____icult (f)
7   di_____er (n)
8   m_____t (e)
9   su_____er (m)
10 w_____kend (e)

c Complete the email from a student with words from Exercises 1 and 3b.

Hi!

Here I am at my new ¹ _____ ! It's good! I have ² _____ every day except Wednesday. My courses aren't ³ _____ . I usually do about two essays every week. I often go out with my ⁴ _____ in the evenings. They're great. Let's ⁵ _____ and play tennis one day. How about next ⁶ _____ ?

Joana

4 Write an email to a friend about your new job or your new course. Include a suggestion to meet.

5 Check your email. Check the spelling.

6 Work in pairs. Exchange emails. Reply to your partner's email.

8f The London Tube

A Tube driver at work

 above ground (expression) /əˈbʌv graʊnd/

 below ground (expression) /bɪˈləʊ graʊnd/

a **billion** (noun) /ˈbɪljən/ 1,000,000,000

 a **brake** (noun) **brake** (verb) /breɪk/

 a **network** (noun) /ˈnetwɜːk/

a **simulator** (noun) /ˈsɪmjəleɪtə/ a machine for learning to drive or fly

Before you watch

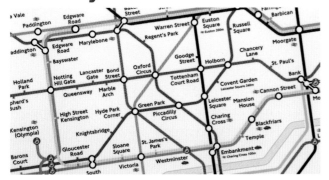

1 Look at the map of the London Tube. Find the stations for these places.

1 Big Ben – *Westminster*
2 Buckingham Palace – *Green Park*
3 the London Eye – *Embankment*

2 Key vocabulary

a Read the sentences. Match the underlined words (1–4) with the pictures (a–d).

1 The journey to Dover is two hours.
2 Tube trains can carry 800 passengers.
3 'It's open! Push!'
4 Some animals make tunnels.

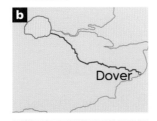

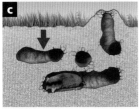

b ▶ 139 Listen and repeat the underlined words.

3 ▶ 140 Look at the word box on page 102. Listen and repeat the words.

While you watch

4 ◨8 Watch the video. Answer the questions.

1 Which underground is the video about?
2 What does Jonny learn to do?

5 ◨8 Watch the first part of the video (0.00–1.00) again. Complete the notes about the Tube with numbers.

1 .... journeys every year
2 .... passengers in 1880
3 .... of the Tube above ground
4 .... metres below ground (some tunnels)
5 .... trains

6 ◨8 Watch the second part of the video again (1.00 to the end). Are the sentences true (T) or false (F)?

1 Matt teaches people to drive trains.
2 The simulator can't change the weather conditions.
3 Jonny practises in snowy weather.
4 Jonny doesn't stop the train correctly.
5 Jonny opens the train doors.

After you watch

7 Complete the paragraph with these verbs. Use the correct present simple form.

have	learn	not / open	practise
stop			

A Tube driver ¹............... to drive in a simulator. The driver ²............... in different conditions. The simulator ³............... the complete London Tube network. At the station, the train ⁴............... in the green area. When the train isn't in the green area, the doors ⁵................. .

8 Work in pairs.
Student A: You are a train driver.
Student B: You are a bus driver.
Prepare answers to these questions.
Then take turns to ask and answer the questions.

• Where do you work?
• What time do you start and finish work?
• Do you like your job?
• What's a typical day like in your job?

Grammar

1 Read about Joel. Write six sentences about him with the underlined words. Use *he*.

Hi. I'm Joel. I'm 46. ¹ I live in New Mexico. I'm a truck driver. ² I have a new job. In my new job, ³ I drive from New Mexico to Arizona every week. That's about 2,400 kilometres. ⁴ I stop every four hours for a break. ⁵ I sleep in my truck. ⁶ In the evenings, I meet other drivers in a snack bar.

2 Rewrite sentences 4, 5 and 6 with these adverbs.

4 usually
5 often
6 sometimes

3 Write questions about Joel with these words.

1 Where / live?
2 What / do?
3 How often / stop?
4 Who / meet?

4 **» MB** Work in pairs. Take turns.
Student A: Ask the questions in Exercise 3.
Student B: Cover the page. Answer the questions.

I CAN	
talk about what people do (present simple)	
say how often people do things (frequency adverbs)	

Vocabulary

5 Read the sentences. Write the job.

1 They take photos.
2 They drive people in cars.
3 They help sick people.
4 They answer questions on the phone.
5 They serve drinks.
6 They help customers in shops.

6 **» MB** Work in pairs. Who works in these places?

1 in a school   4 in a hospital
2 in an office   5 inside
3 in a café   6 outside

7 Complete the words about education.

1 People: classmate, s t _____ ,
   t e _____
2 Places: college, u n _____ ,
   s c _____ , c l _____
3 Things: board, b o _____ , p e ___ ,
   n o _____

I CAN	
talk about jobs and job activities	
talk about education	

Real life

8 Put the phone conversation between a businessman and a receptionist in order.

a Hello.
b Oh. Well, can I speak to her assistant?
c Yes, can I speak to Ms Becker, please?
d Can I help you?
e I'm sorry. She's on holiday this week.
f Good morning, Sports Unlimited. *1*
g OK. Thank you.
h Yes, one moment please.

9 Work in pairs. Practise the conversation in Exercise 8. Change the underlined words.

I CAN	
say why people can't answer a phone call	
make phone calls	

Unit 9 Travel

A passenger shows her passport and train ticket at Machu Picchu village train station, Peru.

FEATURES

1 Work in pairs. Look at the photo. Where are the people?

2 ▶ 141 Listen to four people talk about travel. Write the number of the speaker (1–4) next to the picture.

by boat　　by bus　　by plane　　by train

3 ▶ 141 Listen again. Where do the people go? When do they go?

4 Work in pairs. Ask and answer questions about travel with *where, when* and *how*.

I travel In July.

Where do you go?

I go to Moscow and Kiev.

9a Ready to go

Vocabulary clothes

1 ▶ 142 Look at the photos. Listen and repeat the words.

a pair of boots

a hat

a coat

a top

a jacket

a T-shirt

a skirt

a pair of jeans

a dress

a pair of shoes

a shirt

a pair of trousers

a scarf

a pair of shorts

a jumper

2 Work in pairs. Look at your classmates. Talk about their clothes. Guess their names.

> *A white shirt and a pair of black trousers.*
>
> *Ramon?*
>
> *Yes.*

3 Work in pairs. Talk about your clothes. What do you usually wear

- for work?
- at college?
- at the weekend?
- on holiday?

> *I usually wear a dress for work.*

Reading and listening

4 Read the article by Kate Renshaw. <u>Underline</u> the clothes.

5 Read the article again. What does Kate take with her? What does her sister always take?

6 What do you always take with you when you travel? Tell your partner.

▶ 143

by Kate Renshaw

Ready to go

I'm a travel writer. I usually travel alone. With my passport, money and phone, I'm ready. I take a very small suitcase. But my family sometimes comes with me. And then there are lots of bags. For example, my sister always has two big suitcases. In my sister's suitcases, there are three jackets, lots of jumpers, seven pairs of trousers and lots of tops. There are books too. She never travels without books. In my husband's bag, there's a pair of boots and there are three pairs of shoes! How many pairs of shoes does one man need?

7 ▶ 144 Listen to Kate talk about her next trip. Tick (✓) the things that are in her suitcase.

> a camera
> a laptop
> two shirts
> a skirt
> some books
> a dress
> three scarves
> a pair of shoes
> some T-shirts

Grammar *there is/are*

▶ **THERE IS/ARE**

There's	a	laptop	
There are	two some	shirts T-shirts	in my suitcase.
(there's = there is)			

Now look at page 174.

Two families look at their bags on a trip to Santa Cruz Island, California.

8 Look at the grammar box. Then look at these sentences. Choose the correct option.

1 We use *there's / there are* with singular nouns.
2 We use *there's / there are* with plural nouns.

9 Make sentences with *there's* and *there are* and the things in Exercise 7.

10 Pronunciation *there are*

a ▶ 145 Listen and repeat the sentences with *there are* from Exercise 9. Is the word *are* stressed?

b Work in pairs. Take turns to say true or false sentences about the photo.

> *There are three children.*

> *False. There are two children.*

11 Complete the sentences with *there's* or *there are*. Add extra words or numbers so that the sentences are true for you.

1 _____ a phone in my _____ .
2 _____ people in this class.
3 _____ desks in this room.
4 _____ a book on my desk.
5 _____ a board in this classroom.
6 _____ a computer in my _____ .

Speaking ⟨my life⟩

12 Choose two places you go to for work and on holiday. What do you take with you? Write two lists.

13 Work in pairs. Tell your partner where you go and what you usually take. Use *there's* and *there are*.

> *I often go to Ecuador for work. In my suitcase, there are usually three pairs of trousers. There's a … .*

9b Places to stay

Vocabulary hotel rooms

1 ▶ 146 Look at the photos (1–12). Then listen and repeat the words. Write the words with the photos.

> armchair bath bed chair desk
> fridge lamp shower sofa table
> TV wardrobe

1 ....

2 ....

3 ....

4 ....

5 ....

6 ....

7 ....

8 ....

9 ....

10 ....

11 ....

12 ....

2 Work in pairs. Which things are always in a hotel room? Which things are usually in a hotel room?

> *There's always a bed.*

> *There's usually a fridge.*

Listening

3 Look at the photo below. Who stays in this kind of hotel when they travel?

> business travellers families
> students young couples

4 ▶ 147 Listen to Sandra and Luca plan their trip to Cape Town. Do they want a cheap hotel or an expensive hotel?

5 ▶ 147 Listen again. Read Luca's questions and <u>underline</u> the words he uses.

1 Are there any hotels near the *airport / beach*?
2 Is there a cheap hotel *in the city centre / near the airport*?
3 Is there *a bus / a train* to the city centre?

The Cape Grace Hotel
Victoria Alfred, Cape Town

Grammar *there is/are* negative and question forms

► **THERE IS/ARE NEGATIVE and QUESTION FORMS**

There **isn't**	a train.	
There **aren't**	**any** cheap hotels.	
Is there	a cheap hotel?	Yes, there **is**. No, there **isn't**.
Are there	**any** hotels?	Yes, there **are**. No, there **aren't**.

Now look at page 174.

7 Look at the grammar box. Then look at these sentences. Choose the correct option.

1 We use *a / any* after *there isn't* and *Is there*.
2 We use *a / any* after *there aren't* and *Are there*.

8 Complete the sentences and questions with *a* or *any*.

1 Are there _____ taxis?
2 Is there _____ TV?
3 There aren't _____ trains at night.
4 Is there _____ shower or _____ bath?
5 Are there _____ people in the café?
6 There isn't _____ lamp next to the bed.

9 Put the words in order to make questions and negative sentences.

1 drinks / are / in the fridge / any / there / ?
   Are there any drinks in the fridge?
2 in the room / aren't / chairs / there / any / .
3 a sofa / there / in our room / is / ?
4 near / an airport / there / the coast / isn't / .
5 a train / there / the airport / is / from / ?
6 there / beaches / near / any / the hotel / are / ?

Speaking and writing   my life

10 Work in pairs. Tell your partner the name of your hometown or a place you know. Write questions about your partner's town. Use *Is there a/an … ? / Are there any … ?*

airport nice beach cheap restaurants expensive hotels good hotels tourist attractions	in near	the city/town the centre

11 Work in pairs. Ask and answer your questions from Exercise 10.

Are there any good hotels near the centre?

Yes, there are. There are some four-star hotels and some five-star hotels.

12 Write true sentences with the information from Exercise 11. Use affirmative and negative forms.

13 Work in pairs. Choose a hotel.
Student A: Turn to page 154.
Student B: Turn to page 156.

9c Across a continent

Reading

1 Work in pairs. Look at the map and the photos on page 111. What things do you think you can see or do on a trip across Russia?

2 Read the article on page 111 and check your ideas from Exercise 1. Find the places in the article on the map.

3 Read the article again. Are the sentences true (T) or false (F)?

1 There's a road from Moscow to Vladivostok.
2 You can't sleep on the train from Moscow to Vladivostok.
3 You can leave the train and visit the cities.
4 There aren't any towns near Lake Baikal.
5 The Trans-Siberian Highway finishes in Novosibirsk.

4 Work in pairs. Is this the kind of trip you like? What do you like?

I love trips to different countries.

I like beach holidays.

Vocabulary travel

5 Match a verb in A with words in B. Then check your answers in the article.

A	B
buy	a bus
drive	by train
fly	home
take	cities
travel	a car
visit	tickets

6 Complete the questions with verbs from Exercise 5. Work in pairs. Ask and answer the questions.

1 How often do you _____ by train?
2 Do you _____ a big car?
3 Do you usually _____ tickets online?
4 How often do you _____ different cities?
5 Do you often _____ a bus to work?
6 Is there an airport near your home town? Can you _____ from there?

Grammar imperative forms

> ▶ **IMPERATIVE FORMS**
>
> **Buy** your tickets before your trip.
> **Don't wait** until you get to Moscow.
> (don't = do not)
>
> Now look at page 174.

7 Look at the grammar box. Are the words in bold nouns or verbs?

8 Give tips to a traveller in Russia. Complete the sentences with the imperative form. Use the verbs from the article on page 111.

1 _____ non-stop in seven days.
2 _____ to other passengers.
3 _____ some words in Russian.
4 _____ in hotels.
5 _____ the big cities.
6 _____ by the Trans-Siberian Highway.
7 Don't _____ .

Writing and speaking my life

9 Work in pairs. Write five tips for travellers in your country or a country you know. Think of reasons for the tips.
Don't travel by bus.

10 Work in groups of four. Discuss your tips. Ask follow-up questions.

Don't travel by bus.

Why?

The buses are very slow.

▶ 148

Across a continent *by train* and *by road*

Russia is a very big country. It's 9,000 kilometres from Moscow to Vladivostok and you can travel by train and by road.

BY TRAIN: **THE TRANS-SIBERIAN RAILWAY**

Trains leave Moscow almost every day. Buy your tickets before your trip – don't wait until you get to Moscow. There are two kinds of trip:

You can travel non-stop in seven days. You sleep and eat on the train. You can talk to other passengers. You can learn some words in Russian. You can look at beautiful views.

You can stop and stay in hotels. You can visit the big cities. In Novosibirsk – the main city in Siberia – there are interesting museums, art galleries and theatres. There's also a famous opera house in the city centre. From the towns of Irkutsk or Ulan-Ude, you can take a bus or train to Lake Baikal. This is a UNESCO World Heritage site. Lake Baikal is 636 kilometres long and there are only four or five towns near it. The lake is a great place for sports activities.

BY ROAD: **THE TRANS-SIBERIAN HIGHWAY**

Do you like exciting trips? Then go by the Trans-Siberian Highway. Some people drive their car and some people hitch-hike with Russian drivers.

When you finally get to Vladivostok, you can fly home. Or don't stop – there's a boat from Vladivostok to Japan every week.

hitch-hike (verb) /hɪtʃˈhaɪk/ to travel for free in a car or lorry

A lorry passes hitch-hikers in Tuva, in central Russia.

9d At the hotel

Vocabulary hotels

1 Complete the sentences with these words.

| café | car park | gift shop | restaurant |
| swimming pool | wi-fi | | |

1 You can have dinner in the _____ .
2 You can go online with _____ .
3 You can buy presents in the _____ .
4 You can have a sandwich in the
  _____ .
5 You can park your car in the _____ .
6 You can go swimming in the
  _____ .

2 Work in pairs. Add one more thing to sentences 1–4 in Exercise 1.

Real life requests

3 ▶149 Listen to a conversation between a receptionist and two guests in a hotel. Find:

1 the number of nights
2 the number of the room
3 the opening times of the restaurant
4 the wi-fi password

4 ▶149 Listen again. Match the requests (1–4) with the responses (a–d).

1 We'd like a room for two nights.
2 Can I have your name, please? And a credit card?
3 I'd like help with these bags.
4 Can you tell me the wi-fi password?

a That's no problem.
b Certainly
c Of course.
d Here you are.

> **▶ REQUESTS**
>
> We'd like a room for two nights.
> I'd like help with these bags.
> Can I have your name, please?
> Can you call a taxi, please?
> Certainly.
> Here you are.
> Of course.
> That's no problem.

5 Look at the expressions for REQUESTS. Which question is a request for information?

6 Pronunciation *I'd like, We'd like*

a ▶150 Listen and repeat three sentences from the conversation.

b Work in pairs. Practise these requests. Use *I'd like …* or *We'd like … .*

> a different room
> lunch in our room
> help with the wi-fi
> the key for our room
> our breakfast before 7 am
> a taxi to the airport

> *I'd like a
> different room.*   *That's no problem.*

7 Work in pairs. Look at the audioscript on page 188. Practise the conversation.

8 Work in pairs. Practise the conversation in Exercise 7.

my life ▶ THINGS IN MY SUITCASE ▶ HOTELS ▶ TRAVEL TIPS ▶ **REQUESTS** ▶ TRAVEL ADVICE

9e A great place for a weekend

Writing travel advice

1 Read the advice on a travel website. Answer the questions.

  1 What's the name of the city?
  2 How can you travel there?
  3 Where can you eat?
  4 What can you eat?
  5 What can you see?
  6 What can you do?

2 Read the advice again. <u>Underline</u> four tips from Dani.

3 Writing skill *because*

a Look at the sentence from the text. Find two more sentences with *because*.

> Lisbon is a great place for a weekend trip because there is a lot to see and do!

b Rewrite these sentences with *because*.

  1 Go in spring. It's very hot in summer.
  2 Travel by bus. It's cheap.
  3 Choose your hotel in advance. It's a very popular place.
  4 You can take a boat trip. It's on a river.

4 Make notes about a place you know. Use the questions in Exercise 1.

5 Use your notes and write two or three paragraphs of advice for travellers to the place. Include at least one tip.

6 Check your advice. Check the spelling, punctuation and verbs.

7 Work in pairs. Exchange advice. Is your partner's place a good place to travel to?

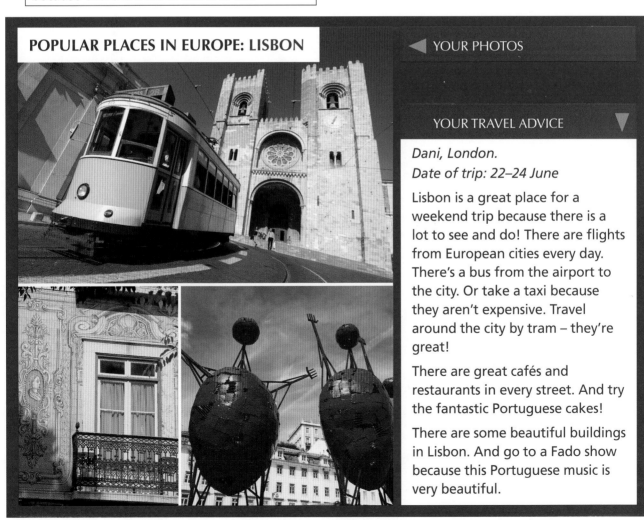

POPULAR PLACES IN EUROPE: LISBON

◀ YOUR PHOTOS

YOUR TRAVEL ADVICE ▼

Dani, London.
Date of trip: 22–24 June

Lisbon is a great place for a weekend trip because there is a lot to see and do! There are flights from European cities every day. There's a bus from the airport to the city. Or take a taxi because they aren't expensive. Travel around the city by tram – they're great!

There are great cafés and restaurants in every street. And try the fantastic Portuguese cakes!

There are some beautiful buildings in Lisbon. And go to a Fado show because this Portuguese music is very beautiful.

9f The people of the reindeer

A Sami man with his reindeer

Before you watch

1 Look at the photo on page 114. What are the animals?

2 Look at the map. Which part of the world is this?

3 Read about the Sami people. Answer the questions.

1 Where are they from?
2 What does *eallin* mean?

The people of the reindeer

The Sami people live in Norway, Sweden, Finland and Russia. They are the 'people of the reindeer'. Traditional Sami people move from place to place with their animals. When they travel, they live in tents. Reindeer are very important to the Sami people. In the Sami language the word for 'a group of reindeer' is *eallu* and the word for 'life' is *eallin*.

4 Key vocabulary

a Read the sentences. Match the underlined words (1–3) with the pictures (a–c).

1 <u>Cut</u> the cake in two.
2 This chair is <u>hard</u>.
3 I like this. It's <u>soft</u>.

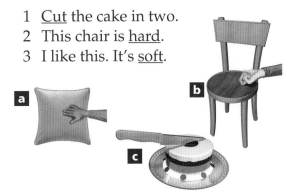

b ▶ 151 Listen and repeat the <u>underlined words</u>.

5 ▶ 152 Look at the word box. Listen and repeat the words.

While you watch

6 🎥 9 These sentences describe scenes in the video. Watch the video and put the scenes in order.

a a man sits with his dog
b a man cuts a piece of bread
c there's snow on the ground *1*
d there's a person in a tent
e a woman works near a house
f a young child laughs
g a young couple sit in a room

7 🎥 9 Watch the video again. Read these sentences about the Sami. Tick (✓) the things you can see in the video.

1 When they travel with the reindeer, the Sami cook their food on a fire.
2 Some young people wear traditional clothes.
3 Reindeer meat and bread are traditional Sami foods.
4 Reindeer eat food under the snow.
5 Children go with their parents on the journey.
6 The Sami people have dogs.

After you watch

8 Can you remember?

1 What type of snow is good for the reindeer?
2 What does the man with the dog say?

9 Complete the sentences about the Sami people in your own words.

1 The Sami are from …
2 They travel …
3 On the journey, …

10 Do you think the Sami way of life is easy or difficult? Why?

 a **couple**
(noun)
/ˈkʌpəl/

 a **fire**
(noun)
/faɪə/

Grammar

1 Look at the photo. Complete the questions with *Is there / Are there*.

1 _____ a map?
2 _____ a passport?
3 _____ books?
4 _____ hat?
5 _____ a camera?
6 _____ tickets?

2 Work in pairs. Ask and answer the questions in Exercise 1. Take turns.

3 ▶▶ MB Work in pairs. Look at the photo for ten seconds. Test your memory. Take turns.
Student A: Read out a sentence.
Student B: Say true or false.

1 There isn't a map.
2 There's a bottle of water.
3 There are some books.
4 There's a pair of glasses.
5 There isn't a pair of boots.
6 There aren't any bags.

4 Put the words in order and write tips.

1 online / the / buy / tickets
2 summer clothes / you / take / with
3 night / travel / don't / at
4 winter / in / go / don't
5 cafés / try / local / the
6 stay / hotel / this / don't / in

I CAN	
use *there is* and *there are* correctly	
give instructions (imperative forms)	

Vocabulary

5 Which clothes are logical? Circle the logical options.

1 In cold weather, I wear *a pair of shorts / a coat / a pair of boots / a hat*.
2 In hot weather, I wear *a T-shirt / a pair of shorts / a skirt / a jacket*.
3 At home, I wear *a jumper / a scarf / a pair of jeans / a top*.
4 In the office, I wear *a pair of trousers / a hat / a shirt / a pair of shoes*.

6 ▶▶ MB Work in pairs. Talk about what you wear every day and at the weekend.

7 Put the letters in order to make words for things in a hotel room.

1 c h a r r m i a _____
2 a b h t _____
3 r i h c a _____
4 m l p a _____
5 r o h s w e _____
6 f o a s _____

I CAN	
talk about clothes	
talk about hotel rooms	
talk about travelling	

Real life

8 Complete the requests in a hotel (1–4). Then match the requests with the responses (a–d).

1 We'd like a _____ for tonight.
2 I'd like help with my _____ .
3 Can you tell me the wi-fi _____ ?
4 Can you _____ a taxi?

a Yes, of course. What time do you want it?
b Here you are. It's on this card.
c That's no problem. What are your names?
d Certainly, sir. Just one moment.

9 Work in pairs. Practise the requests and responses in Exercise 8.

I CAN	
make and respond to requests	

Unit 10 Famous people

Ayrton Senna
in 1994

FEATURES

1 ▶153 Work in pairs. Look at the photo of Ayrton Senna. Listen and write his job and his nationality.

2 ▶154 Listen and repeat the years. Match the years with the people.

1918–2013	Angela Merkel
1940–1980	Ayrton Senna
1942–present	Isabel Allende
1954–present	John Lennon
1960–1994	Malala Yousafzai
1997–present	Nelson Mandela

3 ▶155 Listen and check your answers from Exercise 2.

4 Work in pairs. Choose and write five important years in a list. Dictate these years to your partner. Then compare your lists.

10a Famous 'firsts'

Reading

1 Work in pairs. Look at the photos in the quiz *Explorers*. What do the people have in common?

2 ▶ 156 Read the quiz. Complete the sentences with the names. Listen and check.

Grammar *be: was/were*

> **BE: WAS/WERE**

I/He/She/It	**was**	an explorer. Russian.
You/We/You/They	**were**	from Russia.

Now look at page 176.

3 Look at the grammar box. <u>Underline</u> these past forms of *be* in the texts (1–4). Then match the texts with four of the people in the quiz.

1 She was born in **1939**. She was in a team of Japanese mountaineers. They were all women.

2 He was born in **1480**. He was Portuguese, but he was an explorer for the Spanish king Carlos I.

3 She was born in the United States on **29 September 1955**. She was the leader of an expedition to the South Pole in **1993**. All the people on the expedition were women.

4 He was from Norway and he was born on **16 July 1872**. His parents were rich. His father was a sea captain.

Explorers

Ferdinand Magellan

Yuri Gagarin

Roald Amundsen

Junko Tabei

Ann Bancroft

Valentina Tereshkova

Do you know these famous explorers? Match their names with the expeditions.

• The first round-the-world expedition was from 1519 to 1522. The expedition captain was ....

• The first successful South Pole expedition was in 1911. The expedition leader was ....

• The first man in space was .... The first woman in space was .... They were both from Russia.

• The first woman at the top of Everest was .... on 16 May 1975.

• The first woman at the North Pole was .... on 1 May 1986.

a **captain** (noun) /ˈkæptɪn/ the leader of a ship or plane
an **expedition** (noun) /ˌekspəˈdɪʃən/ a trip with scientists and/or explorers
the **North Pole** (noun) /ˌnɔːθ ˈpəʊl/
the **South Pole** (noun) /ˌsaʊθ ˈpəʊl/

North Pole
South Pole

4 Choose the correct option.

1 I *was/were* born in Kuala Lumpur.
2 My parents *was/were* born in London.
3 My father *was/were* born in 1970.
4 My mother *was/were* born in 1971.

5 Complete the paragraphs with *was* and *were*.

Yuri Gagarin [1] _____ born in 1934. His parents [2] _____ farmers. From 1955 to 1961, he [3] _____ a pilot. The first space rockets [4] _____ small and so the first people in space [5] _____ small too. Gagarin [6] _____ a small man – 1.57 metres.

Valentina Tereshkova [7] _____ born in central Russia in 1937. Her parents [8] _____ from Belarus. She [9] _____ a factory worker.

After their trips into space, on 12 April 1961 and 16 June 1963, Gagarin and Tereshkova [10] _____ famous all over the world.

6 Pronunciation *was/were* weak forms

a ▶157 Listen and repeat three sentences from Exercise 5.

b Write three sentences about Valentina Tereshkova. Read them to your partner. Are they the same?

Vocabulary dates

7 Look at the *Important dates in exploration*. Complete the dates with information from the quiz *Explorers*.

Important dates in exploration	
1st _____	first woman at the North Pole
2nd June 1953	news of first men at the top of Everest
3rd November 1957	Sputnik II into space
4th October 1957	Sputnik I into space
5th / 6th / 7th / 8th / 9th / 10th / 11th	
12th April 1961	first man in space
13th December 1972	last man on the moon
14th December 1911	first people at the South Pole
15th	
16th _____	first woman at the top of Everest
17th / 18th / 19th	
20th July 1969	first men on the moon

8 ▶158 Look at the *Important dates in exploration*. Listen and repeat the ordinal numbers.

9 ▶159 Listen and repeat the dates. What words do we use with the ordinal numbers?

'the first of May 1986'

10 Work in pairs. Look at the *Important dates in exploration*. Take turns.
Student A: Say a date.
Student B: Say the event.

the first of May 1986

the first woman at the North Pole

11 ▶160 Say these ordinal numbers. Listen and check.

21st	22nd	23rd	24th
25th	26th	27th	28th
29th	30th	31st	

Speaking my life

12 Work in pairs. What are three important dates in your country?

The 14th of July is Bastille Day.

13 Work in pairs.
Student A: Dictate three important dates from your past to your partner.
Student B: Say the dates.
Student A: Say why the date was important.

1 September 1990

It was my first day at school.

10b People I remember

Listening

1 Work in pairs. Who was your best friend when you were young? Is he/she your best friend now?

2 Read the information about the radio programme. Answer the questions.

1 When's the programme on the radio?
2 What's the programme about?
3 Who's on the programme today?

3 ▶161 Listen to Joe and Aneta. Complete the sentences with these words.

| a writer | animals | *Frankenstein* | meerkats |
| on TV | reading | | |

1 Joe loves _____ .
2 David Attenborough was _____ .
3 Joe's favourite programme was about
  _____ .
4 Aneta loves _____ .
5 Mary Shelley was _____ .
6 _____ was by Mary Shelley.

4 ▶161 Listen again. Choose the correct answer to the interviewer's questions.

1 Was he on TV?
  Yes, he was. / No, he wasn't.
2 Were the programmes only for children?
  Yes, they were. / No, they weren't.
3 Were you good at English?
  Yes, I was. / No, I wasn't.

5 Work in pairs. What were you good at at school? Tell your partner and answer questions.

> *Were you good at English at school?*

> *Yes, I was.*

People I remember

Radio 6 19.30 13 March

In this programme, we remember people who were important to us when we were young. We talk to Joe, Aneta and Olga about a TV star, a writer and an Olympic champion.

Grammar *be: was/were* negative and question forms

▶ **BE: WAS/WERE NEGATIVE and QUESTION FORMS**

I/He/She/It You/We/You/They	wasn't weren't	on TV. famous.
Was **Were**	I/he/she/it you/we/you/they	on TV? famous?

Yes, No, Yes, No,	I/he/she/it I/he/she/it you/we/you/they you/we/you/they	**was.** **wasn't.** **were.** **weren't.**

Now look at page 176.

6 Look at the grammar box. What are the negative and question forms of *was* and *were*?

7 ▶162 Complete the interview with Olga with *was, were, wasn't* or *weren't*. Listen and check.

I: Olga, who ¹ ___was___ important to you when you were young?

O: I remember Michael Johnson. He was a great sportsman.

I: ² _____ he an Olympic champion?

O: Yes, he ³ _____ . Four times. The last time was in 2000.

I: ⁴ _____ the 2000 Olympics in Beijing?

O: No, they ⁵ _____ . They were in Sydney.

I: ⁶ _____ you good at sports at school?

O: Yes, I ⁷ _____ . I was in the basketball team at school.

8 Complete the questions with *was* or *were*.

1 ___Were___ you on TV?
2 _____ your parents famous?
3 _____ you happy at school?
4 _____ English your favourite subject?
5 _____ your teachers at school nice?
6 _____ your school good?

9 Work in pairs. Think about when you were young. Ask and answer the questions in Exercise 8.

Vocabulary describing people

10 Work in pairs. Look at the words in **bold** in the sentences. Write the name of a person you both know for each word.

1 She's a **famous** actor.　*Meryl Streep*
2 He's a **funny** person.　*Mr Bean*
3 A **popular** person has lots of friends.
4 A **nice** person helps other people.
5 A **clever** person is good at different subjects.
6 An **interesting** person has lots of ideas.

Speaking ⟨ my life ⟩

11 Who was important to you when you were young? Write three names on three pieces of paper. Think about the answers to these questions.
• Who was he/she?
• Why was he/she important to you?

12 Work in groups. Mix the pieces of paper from Exercise 11. Take turns to read a name. Ask and answer the questions about the names.

Who was Monika Gomes?

She was my first teacher. She was funny and nice.

10c The first Americans

Reading

1 Work in pairs. Do you think these sentences are true (T) or false (F)?

1 The Inca Empire was in North America.
2 The Maya people were from Central America.
3 The Aztecs were from Peru.
4 The Apache people were from South America.

2 Read the first paragraph of the article *The first Americans*. Check your answers from Exercise 1.

3 Read the rest of the article. Find:

1 one thing the Incas were famous for
2 two things the Maya people were famous for
3 two Aztec words we use in English
4 two famous rulers
5 a famous Apache

4 Can you remember? Complete the sentences. Then check your answers in the article.

1 There are _____ countries in North, Central and South America.
2 The Inca roads were on the _____ coast of South America.
3 The Mayan number _____ was a dot.
4 _____ was born in 1829.

5 Who were important leaders in your country's history?

Grammar regular past simple verbs

▶ **REGULAR PAST SIMPLE VERBS**

I/You He/She/It We/You/They	**lived** in Central America. **died** in 1903.

Now look at page 176.

6 Look at the grammar box. Answer the questions.

1 What is the infinitive of the verbs?
2 What letter do we add to these verbs to make the regular past simple form?

7 Work in pairs. Write true sentences.

was born lived died	in Germany / in the United States in Pakistan in Liverpool / in New York in South Africa in Poland / in France in Peru / in Chile

Albert Einstein was born in Germany and he died in the United States.

Albert Einstein   Isabel Allende   John Lennon

Malala Yousafzai   Marie Curie   Nelson Mandela

Speaking (my life)

8 Work in pairs. Choose four famous people. Find information about when and where they were born, lived and died. Why were they famous?

9 Work with a new partner. Take turns to give the details of the people. Can you guess the names of your partner's people?

He was born in London in 1947. He died in New York in January 2016. He was a singer. Who was he?

David Bowie?

Yes!

▶ **163**

THE FIRST AMERICANS

First Nations and Native Americans

The Aztec Empire until about 1580

The Maya

The Inca Empire until 1532

Geronimo: Apache hero
16 June 1829 – 17 February 1909

There are now twenty-three countries and twenty-three nationalities in North, Central and South America. In the past, there were different groups of people in America. The Inca people lived in a large area of South America. The Maya people lived in Central America. And people in Mexico were part of the Aztec empire. In North America, the Apache, the Navajo, the Sioux and other Native American groups lived in different areas.

The Inca empire was famous for its roads. There were roads on the west coast of South America, from the north to the south. The Maya people were famous for their writing and maths systems. In Mayan maths, a dot was 'one' and a bar was 'five'. The capital city of the Aztecs was Tenochtitlan. Mexico City is in the same place. The words *chocolate* and *tomato* were Aztec words.

Famous rulers in South America were Tupac Amaru, an Inca ruler, and Moctezuma, an Aztec ruler. One famous Apache was Geronimo, but he wasn't a ruler. Geronimo was born on 16 June 1829. When he was a young man, there was a war between the USA and Native Americans. Geronimo was a war hero. He died in 1909.

a **bar** (noun) /bɑː/ ▬
a **dot** (noun) /dɒt/ ●
a **hero** (noun) /hɪərəʊ/ a person who's not afraid
a **war** (noun) /wɔː(r)/ conflict. For example: World War I (1914–1918).

10d I'm sorry

Vocabulary activities

1 Look at the photos. Write the letters (a–f) with the words.

At nine o'clock yesterday I was …

1 on a train	4 in traffic
2 at home	5 not well
3 busy	6 on the phone

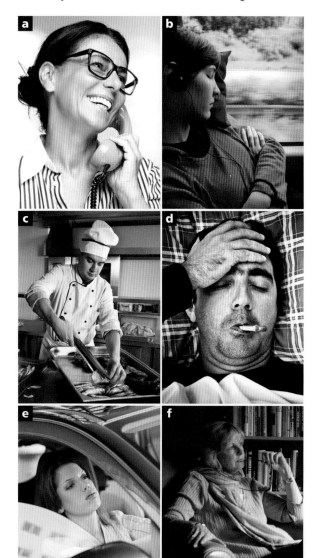

2 Work in pairs. Ask and answer questions.

Were you at home at nine o'clock yesterday?

Yes, I was.

No, I wasn't.

Real life apologizing

3 ▶ 164 Listen to three conversations. Write the number of the conversation (1–3) next to the places.

a in a café
b in a classroom
c in an office

4 ▶ 164 Look at the expressions for APOLOGIZING. Listen again and write the numbers (1–3) with the expressions. Two expressions are in two conversations.

▶ APOLOGIZING	
I'm (very) sorry.	We weren't at home.
I'm sorry I'm late.	It's OK.
The train was late.	That's OK.
I was (very) busy.	Don't worry.

5 Pronunciation sentence stress

a ▶ 165 Listen and repeat these sentences. <u>Underline</u> the word with the main stress.

1 I'm sorry I'm late.
2 The train was late.
3 I was very busy.
4 We weren't at home.

b Work in pairs. Practise the conversations. Pay attention to sentence stress.

6 Work in pairs. Practise the conversations again. Use the vocabulary in Exercise 1.

Hello.

Hi, I'm sorry I'm late. I was in traffic.

That's OK.

my life ▶ DATES AND EVENTS ▶ PEOPLE IN MY PAST ▶ WHO WAS HE/SHE? ▶ APOLOGIZING
▶ AN EMAIL

10e Sorry!

Writing an email

1 Read the emails (1–3). Which two are apologies? Which one expresses sympathy?

2 Read the emails again. Answer the questions.

1   Where was Marc yesterday?
2   Who wasn't well last week?
3   What information does Ms Braun need?

---

1 Hi Jon

I'm very sorry about yesterday. I was in meetings all day. It's very busy at work. See you tonight?

Love

Marc

---

2 Dear Victoria

I'm sorry you weren't well last week. Are you better now? Hope to see you tomorrow!

Best wishes

Simone

---

3 Dear Ms Braun

I apologize for the delay in this reply. I attach the information about our prices.

Best regards

Andres Pires

---

3 Writing skill expressions in emails

a Look at the expressions in the emails in Exercise 1. Complete the table.

Starting an email	Ending an email
Dear …	All the best
....	....
	....
	....

b Which expressions are best for emails to friends? Which expressions are best for work or business emails?

c Complete the emails with expressions from the table in Exercise 3a. There is more than one option.

---

1 .... Mr Bruni

I'm very sorry I wasn't in the office yesterday. I hope to see you on your next visit.

2 ....

Carlos Morales

---

3 .... Fran

I wasn't well at the weekend. I'm sorry I wasn't at your party. Was it fun? I hope so.

4 ....

Jack

---

4 Write two emails. Check your expressions.

1   You weren't at a meeting because your train was very late. Apologize to your boss.
2   Your friend was in hospital at the weekend. Express sympathy.

5 Work as a class. Exchange emails with two classmates. Write a short reply to the emails you receive.

Old computers

A computer from
the 1980s

Before you watch

1 Work in pairs. What was your first computer?

2 Key vocabulary

a Read the sentences. Match the underlined words (1–4) with the pictures (a–d).

1 Do you use a <u>mouse</u> with your laptop?
2 How do I <u>turn on</u> this machine?
3 Where's the light <u>switch</u>?
4 First, <u>press</u> 'enter' on the keyboard.

b ▶ 166 Listen and repeat the underlined words.

3 ▶ 167 Look at the word box. Listen and repeat the words.

While you watch

4 🎞 10 Watch the video. Tick (✓) the things that surprise the kids.

1 The computer is very big.
2 The switch is on the back.
3 There isn't a camera.
4 There aren't any apps.
5 There isn't any internet.

5 🎞 10 Watch the first part (0.00–0.33) of the video again. Match the names with the comments.

1 Krischelle   a Where do you put this?
2 Dylan   b It's huge.
3 Jayka   c It looks cool.

6 🎞 10 Watch the second part of the video (0.33 to the end) again. Tick (✓) the things the kids try to do.

1 turn the computer on
2 write their names
3 play games
4 send a message
5 go on the internet

7 🎞 10 Watch the second part of the video again. Complete the kids' questions.

1 How do I _____ this?
2 Why does it have to make so much _____ ?
3 Where's the _____ ?
4 Are there any _____ on it?

After you watch

8 Can you remember?

1 What year was the computer from?
2 What was the first thing you need to do on the computer?

9 Complete the sentences about the early 1980s with *was, wasn't, were* or *weren't*.

1 Computers _____ very big.
2 There _____ any internet.
3 There _____ any websites.
4 Computer games _____ very basic.
5 What colour _____ the writing on the old computer?
6 Who _____ Tim Berners-Lee?

10 Work in pairs. Tell your partner the date of:

1 your first computer
2 your first phone
3 your first social media post

---

boxy (adjective) / ˈbɒksi/ in the shape of a box

huge (adjective) /hjuːdʒ/ very, very big

a **button** (noun) /ˈbʌtən/

a **monitor** (noun) /ˈmɒnɪtə/

go ahead (verb) /ˈgəʊ əhed/ to start

a **(computer) programme** (noun) /ˈprəʊgræm/ an app

Grammar

1 Complete the article with *was* or *were*.

Sam Sunderland: the first British winner of the *Dakar Rally*

In 2017, Sam Sunderland ¹ _____ the first British winner of the *Dakar Rally*. He ² _____ on a motorbike. Sam ³ _____ born in 1989 and his first win in a motorbike race ⁴ _____ in 2010. The winner of the car group in 2017 ⁵ _____ Stéphane Peterhansel. He and his co-driver are French. They ⁶ _____ also the winners in 2016.

2 Complete the questions with *was* or *were*.

1 Who _____ the first British winner of the Dakar Rally?
2 When _____ Sam Sunderland born?
3 Who _____ the winners of the car group in 2016?

3 **≫ MB** Work in pairs. Take turns.
Student A: Ask the questions in Exercise 2.
Student B: Cover the page. Answer the questions.

4 **≫ MB** Work in pairs. How many famous people can you name who:

1 were from your home city?
2 lived in your country?
3 died last year?

I CAN	
talk about the past (*was/were*)	
use *lived* and *died* correctly (past simple)	

Vocabulary

5 Complete the dates in the sentences with these words.

in	in	of	on	the

1 I was born on the third _____ June.
2 My sister was born _____ 1987.
3 My wife was born on _____ eleventh of September.
4 My son was born _____ April.
5 My father was born _____ the second of January, 1959.

6 Choose the correct option.

1 My first boss was very *nice* / *great*.
2 My sister is always *funny* / *famous*.
3 When I was a child, I wasn't *clever* / *funny* at maths.
4 That band is *famous* / *nice* here.
5 Our science teacher was *interesting* / *popular* with her students.

7 **≫ MB** Work in pairs. Say the last time you were:

at home	in traffic	on a train
busy	not well	on the phone

I CAN	
say dates	
describe people (adjectives)	
talk about activities	

Real life

8 Put the conversation in order.

a Don't worry. Are you OK now?
b Hello, Carolyn.   *1*
c Hi. Where were you this morning?
d Oh! I'm sorry. I wasn't well.
e The boss was here at nine o'clock.
f Why?
g Yes, thanks.

9 Work in pairs. Practise the conversation in Exercise 8.

I CAN	
make and accept apologies	

Unit 11 True stories

FEATURES

1 Work in pairs. Look at the photo. Which do you think is the correct caption for the photo?

a A man reads the newspaper in Timbuktu.
b In Timbuktu, a man looks at documents about his family.
c A man in Timbuktu writes a letter to his son.

2 ▶ 168 Listen and check your idea from Exercise 1.

3 ▶ 168 Listen again and complete the sentences.

1 Timbuktu was a centre of learning for .... of years.
2 Lots of the books and documents were in libraries and family ....
3 Some books are .... hundred years old.

4 What's your favourite book? Tell the class.

11a 'Ötzi' the Iceman

Reading

1 Read the article about 'Ötzi' the Iceman. Answer the questions.

1 Where were the tourists from?
2 Where were they in September 1991?
3 Where was the body?
4 What kind of investigation was it?

2 Read the article again. <u>Underline</u> these past forms in the article. Then write the past forms next to the infinitives (1–6).

was/were	went	saw	came	took	had

1 be .... *was/were*
2 come ....
3 go ....
4 have ....
5 see ....
6 take ....

Grammar irregular past simple verbs

▶ **IRREGULAR PAST SIMPLE VERBS**

I/You He/She/(It) We/You/They	**went** *for a walk.* **saw** *a body.*

Now look at page 178.

3 Look at the grammar box. Then look at this sentence. Choose the correct option.

Irregular past simple verbs *end / don't end* with *-ed*.

4 Complete the sentences with these irregular past simple verbs.

came	had	saw	took	went

1 Last summer we .... to Italy.
2 We .... some beautiful places.
3 We .... lots of photos.
4 We .... a great time.
5 We .... home after three weeks.

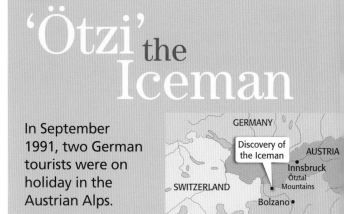

▶ 169

'Ötzi' the Iceman

In September 1991, two German tourists were on holiday in the Austrian Alps.

They went for a walk and they saw a body in the ice. The body was very old – it wasn't the body of a climber or walker. There was a knife and a bag with the body. The police came and they took the body to the University of Innsbruck in Austria.

The police had many questions about the body. Was it a man or a woman? Where was he or she from? How old was the body? But this wasn't a police investigation. It was a scientific investigation.

Listening

5 ▶ 170 Listen to more information about the investigation. Complete the sentences.

1 Ötzi lived about .... years ago.
2 Ötzi was about .... years old when he died.

6 ▶ 170 Listen again. Match the two parts of the sentences.

1 The scientists at the University of Innsbruck started
2 They called him 'Ötzi' because
3 The scientists finished
4 The scientists think an arrow killed

a Ötzi.
b the body was in the Ötztal mountains.
c their investigation.
d their report about Ötzi.

The Iceman at the South Tyrol Museum of Archaeology in Bolzano, Italy

The Iceman's knife

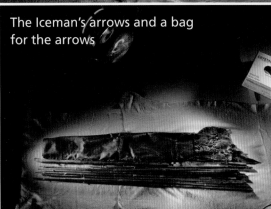

The Iceman's arrows and a bag for the arrows

7 <u>Underline</u> six regular past simple verbs in Exercises 5 and 6. What are the infinitives of these verbs?

8 Complete the sentences. Use the past simple form of the verb.

1 My friend _walked_ (walk) across the Alps in 2016.
2 I _____ (start) my English course last year.
3 My mother _____ (live) in Italy from 2009 to 2015.
4 Our holiday _____ (finish) last Sunday.
5 My mother _____ (be) on a plane with Meryl Streep.
6 We _____ (see) a great film last week.
7 I _____ (have) an exam yesterday.

9 **Pronunciation -*ed* regular past simple verbs**

a ▶ 171 Listen to the infinitive and past simple form of these verbs. Which verb has an extra syllable?

1 call   called
2 die   died
3 finish   finished
4 kill   killed
5 live   lived
6 start   started

b ▶ 172 Listen and repeat the regular past simple sentences from Exercise 8.

Speaking ⟨ my life ⟩

10 Make true and false sentences about you and your family or friends with past simple verbs. Read your sentences to your partner. Can you find the false sentences?

My parents walked to the South Pole in 2012.

I think that's false!

11 Work in pairs. Can you remember the story of Ötzi? Tell the story with these verbs. Take turns with each sentence.

went	saw	came	took
had	started	called	finished
killed			

11b Life stories

Vocabulary life events

1 Complete the paragraph with the life events. What are the infinitives of the verbs?

left school	studied
lived	was born
met my husband	went to school
started work	

I ¹ .... in 1987. I
² .... at 3 Princes Street
with my family. My sister and I
³ .... in our village. When
I was eighteen, I ⁴ ....
I ⁵ .... mathematics at
university in Liverpool. I
⁶ .... when I was twenty-
three and I ⁷ .... at work.

2 Write true sentences about you with the verbs in Exercise 1.

3 Work in pairs. Read your sentences to your partner. What do you have in common?

Listening

4 Read about Caroline Gerdes. Answer the questions.

1 Where was she born?
2 Where did she go to school?
3 What does she write about?

Caroline Gerdes is a journalist. She was born in New Orleans, and she lived there and studied there too. She writes about the 'life story' of her city. She talks to people about their lives and their history. She writes about the life and the culture of New Orleans – Mardi Gras, the story of jazz music and other things.

5 ▶ 173 Listen to an interview with Dinah, also from New Orleans. Tick (✓) the life events in Exercise 1 you hear.

Mardi Gras in the city of New Orleans

6 ▶ 173 Listen to the interview again. Put the questions in the order you hear them.

  a Did you study art at university?
  b Did you live there when you were a child?
  c Why did you decide to be a musician?
  d What did you want to be when you were a child?

7 Work in pairs. Test your memory. What is Dinah's answer to the last question?

Grammar past simple negative and question forms

▶ **PAST SIMPLE NEGATIVE and QUESTION FORMS**

I/You He/She/It We/You/They	didn't	study art.
Did	I/you he/she/it we/you/they	live there?
Yes, No,	I/you he/she/it we/you/they	did. didn't.

Now look at page 178.

8 Look at the grammar box. Then look at these sentences. Choose the correct option.

  1 We use the *infinitive / past simple* form of the verb after *did* in questions.
  2 We use the *infinitive / past simple* form of the verb after *didn't*.

9 Put the words in order to make negative sentences and questions.

  1 didn't / at school / English / study / I / .
     I didn't study English at school.
  2 go / university / you / did / to / ?
  3 at work / meet / didn't / we / .
  4 history / study / didn't / Josep / .
  5 London / live / in / they / did / ?
  6 start / Asha / work / did / last year / ?

10 Complete the questions with *Did you* and these verbs. Then listen and check.

go	leave	live	meet	start	~~study~~

  1 *Did you study* English at school?
  2 _____ your best friend at school?
  3 _____ in a big city when you were young?
  4 _____ school when you were eighteen?
  5 _____ work last year?
  6 _____ on holiday every year?

11 Pronunciation *did you … ?*

a ▶ 174 Listen and repeat the questions from Exercise 10.

b Work in pairs. Ask and answer the questions in Exercise 10.

> Did you study English at school?
> Yes, I did.
> No, I didn't.

Speaking ⟨ my life ⟩

12 Work in pairs. Write questions about last week and last year. Then work as a class. Find one name for each question.

  1 see the film *King Kong*
     Did you see the film King Kong last year?
  2 go on holiday
  3 meet a friend
  4 take a bus
  5 finish your homework
  6 start a new job

> Did you see the film King Kong last year?
> Yes, I did. I saw it with two friends.

13 Write six sentences about people in your class with the names.

Lidia saw the film King Kong last year.

11c A problem in Madagascar

Reading

1 Look at the photos and find:

> an animal   a plant   rocks

2 Work in pairs. Do you think these adjectives describe the things in the photos? Which things?

> beautiful   dangerous   fantastic
> interesting   unusual

3 Read the article about a trip to Madagascar. Answer the questions.

1 What does *tsingy* mean in the Malagasy language?
2 When did Neil Shea go to Madagascar?
3 Who did he go with?
4 Why did they go to Madagascar?

4 Read the last paragraph of the article again. Put the events in the correct order.

a Neil Shea went to hospital.
b The nurse asked him a question.
c Neil Shea cut his leg.
d Neil Shea fell.
e The nurse cleaned his leg.

5 Work in pairs. Did the nurse think it was a good idea to go to the *tsingy*?

Grammar past simple *Wh-* questions

▶ PAST SIMPLE *WH-* QUESTIONS

What Where When Why Who	did	I/you/he/she/it we/you/they	do? go? get there? see? meet?

Now look at page 178.

6 Look at the grammar box. Then look at the questions in Exercise 3. Which question words are in Exercise 3?

7 Complete the questions about Neil Shea with the correct *Wh-* word.

1 _When_ did he fall?
2 _____ did he cut?
3 _____ did he go?
4 _____ did he see in hospital?
5 _____ did she say?

8 Work in pairs. Ask and answer the questions in Exercise 7.

9 Word focus *get*

a Look at the sentence from the article. Which sentence (1–4) has the same meaning of *get*?

After five days, we got to the park.

1 Did you get my message?
2 I got a ticket for the plane to Cairo.
3 Can you get a bus from the airport?
4 We got home on Friday.

b Complete the sentences with these words.

> a taxi   a new car   an email
> some bananas   there   to work

1 I got _____ at the market.
2 There wasn't a train, so we got _____ .
3 I usually get _____ at nine o'clock.
4 We got _____ from our friends.
5 What time did you get _____ ?
6 They got _____ last week.

Speaking ⟨ my life ⟩

10 Work in pairs. Choose a day from last week. Ask and answer questions with *Did …* and question words. Find one thing you both did.

> Did you have breakfast?   Yes, I did.

> What did you have?   I had toast and orange juice.

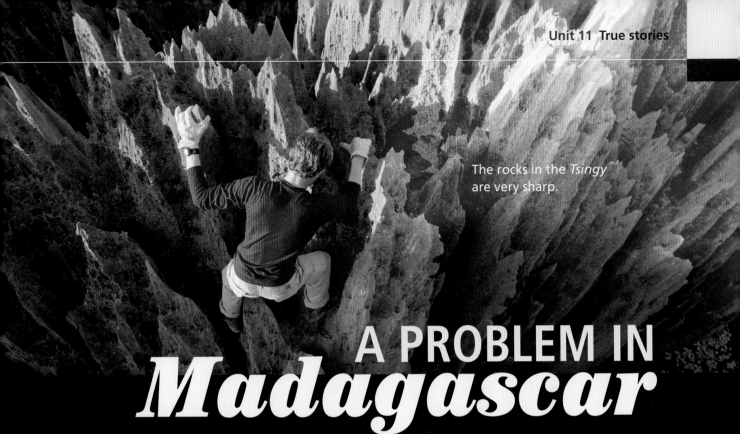

The rocks in the *Tsingy* are very sharp.

A PROBLEM IN
Madagascar

By Neil Shea

▶ 175

Madagascar is a fantastic place. About ninety per cent of the types of animals and plants there live only in Madagascar. There are some very unusual animals and plants in Madagascar's Tsingy de Bemaraha National Park, but it's a dangerous place. The rocks – the 'tsingy' – in the park are very sharp. The word 'tsingy' means 'you can't walk here' in the Malagasy language.

I went to Madagascar in March. It was the end of the rainy season. I was with a scientist and a photographer. We wanted to find some new animals and plants. We travelled to the park with our guide. After five days, we got to the park.

We walked through the *tsingy*. The rocks cut our clothes and our shoes too. It was very dangerous, but we saw hundreds of animals and plants. We saw beautiful birds and unusual white lemurs with red eyes. They didn't have any problems on the *tsingy* rocks!

Then, one afternoon, I fell on a rock. I cut my leg. The cut was very bad and very dirty. We were a long way from a town. After two days, I got to hospitaI. The nurse cleaned my leg. She asked me a question. 'Why did you go to the *tsingy*? Madagascans don't go to the *tsingy* because it's dangerous.' It's true – it is dangerous, but it's also amazing.

sharp (adjective) /ʃɑːp/ A sharp knife can cut things.

There are twenty-three types of this plant in the world. Eighteen of them are only in Madagascar.

This lemur lives only in Madagascar.

Did you have a good time?

Real life talking about the past

1 Work in pairs. Look at the photo. What can you see?

2 ▶ 176 Listen to three conversations. Write the number of the conversation (1–3).

The people …
a had a meal.
b were in Sydney.
c didn't have a holiday.

3 ▶ 176 Listen again and answer the questions for the conversations.

1 Did they go swimming?
2 Did they stay at home?
3 Did they pay for the meal?

4 Pronunciation *didn't*

a ▶ 177 Listen to three sentences from the conversations. Notice how the *t* in *didn't* isn't pronounced.

b ▶ 177 Listen and repeat the sentences.

Vocabulary time expressions

5 Look at these expressions. Which expressions did you hear in the conversations?

on Friday	last weekend
last night	yesterday
last week	last year

6 Work in pairs. Say one thing you did at each time in Exercise 5.

I had a nice meal on Friday.

> ▶ **TALKING ABOUT THE PAST**
>
> Did you have a good holiday last year?
> Did you have a good time in Sydney last week?
> Did you have a nice **meal** last night?
> Why not?
> There was a shark in the sea!
> We didn't go swimming.
> It was delicious.

7 Work in pairs. Look at the audioscript on page 189. Practise the conversations.

8 Work in pairs. First, choose an event for each time. Then take turns to ask and answer questions about the events. Say one thing you didn't do.

a day at the beach	last month
a holiday	last night
a meal	last week
a party	on Saturday
a trip	yesterday

Hi. Did you have a good day at the beach yesterday?

Yes, thanks. I did. But I didn't go in the water.

Why not?

It was very cold!

my life ▷ TRUE OR FALSE? ▷ LAST WEEK AND LAST YEAR ▷ ONE DAY LAST WEEK ▶ **TALKING ABOUT THE PAST**
▷ A LIFE STORY

11e Childhood memories

Writing a life story

1 Work in pairs. Do you read the life stories of famous people? Who?

2 Read about Tyler. Which paragraph (A–C) gives information about these things?

1 toys
2 family
3 school

3 Read about Tyler again and answer the questions.

1 When was Tyler born?
2 Who did he live with?
3 Which toys does he describe?
4 Did he like school?

4 Writing skill *when*

a Complete the sentence from the text.

When I was seven, _____

b Find three more sentences with *When* in the text.

c Rewrite these sentences as one sentence with *When*. Don't forget the comma.

1 My parents were young. They weren't rich.
2 My father was a student. He met my mother.
3 I was a child. I had lots of toys.
4 I was three years old. My sister was born.

5 Make notes about your childhood. Make notes about the things in Exercise 2. Answer the questions in Exercise 3 for yourself.

6 Use your notes and write two or three paragraphs about your childhood memories. Include a sentence with *When*.

7 Check your paragraphs. Check the spelling, punctuation and verbs.

8 Work in pairs. Exchange paragraphs. Find one surprising thing in your partner's paragraphs. Ask two questions about his or her childhood.

MY CHILDHOOD MEMORIES
Tyler

A I was born on 15th July 1995 in Kansas City. When I was a child, I lived with my brother, my parents and my grandfather. My grandfather was funny and interesting. He died in 2010.

B When I was seven, my favourite toy was a red helicopter. I got it from my grandfather. When my friends saw my helicopter, they wanted it. My friend Nathan had a blue bike. I loved it!

C I went to school with my brother every day. We were in the same class because we're twins. I didn't like school very much. When I was sixteen, I left school and I started my first job the next day. That was the end of my childhood.

11f True stories?

Bonfire night in the UK is
on 5th November.

Before you watch

1 Look at the photo and the caption on page 138. What is happening?

2 Key vocabulary

a Read the sentences. Match the underlined words (1–4) with the pictures (a–d).

1 An ambulance took my brother to hospital.
2 We can carry water in a bucket.
3 We have new curtains in the living room.
4 I passed my English test!

ENGLISH TEST
9/10

b ▶ 178 Listen and repeat the underlined words.

3 ▶ 179 Look at the word box. Listen and repeat the words.

4 Work in pairs. What is the infinitive of these past simple verbs?

1 ate	6 knew	11 started
2 cut	7 lit	12 stopped
3 fell	8 opened	13 threw
4 had	9 said	14 took
5 hid	10 sang	15 went

While you watch

5 ☐ 11 In the video, there are four stories. One story is about bonfire night. Look at the four groups of verbs (a–d). Watch the first part of the video (0.00–2.34) and match the groups of verbs with the stories (1–4). Do you think the stories are true or false?

a	started	had	opened	lit	threw
b	sang				
c	had	hid	knew	say	
d	went	fell	cut	stopped	took	ate

6 ☐ 11 Watch the first part of the video again. We don't hear the interviewer's questions. Write the number of the story next to the question.

a Did the teacher find you? ....
b What happened? What did you do? ....
c Did you win? ....
d How long was the journey to hospital? ....

7 ☐ 11 Work in pairs. Do you think the stories are true or false? Watch the second part of the video (2.35 to the end) and check.

After you watch

8 Work in pairs. What can you remember?

1 Was the person in the cupboard a boy or a girl?
2 How did the person in story 2 cut her leg?
3 Did the person in story 3 do well in the competition?
4 What month was it in story 4?

9 Work in pairs. Choose one of the stories. Try to tell the story.

 blood (noun) /blʌd/

hide (verb) /haɪd/ to be in a place where people can't see you

a lie (noun) /laɪ/ the opposite of the truth

 a rainbow (noun) /ˈreɪnbəʊ/

a song (noun) /sɒŋ/ music and words we sing

 throw (verb) /θrəʊ/

Grammar

1 Complete the text with the past simple forms of the verbs.

Field notes

Last month, I was with a group of people on a boat. We ¹_____ (be) in Alaska. Justin Hofman, a scuba diver, ²_____ (be) in the water. He ³_____ (have) a camera. He ⁴_____ (take) pictures under the sea. He ⁵_____ (send) video pictures to us on the boat. It was very exciting! We ⁶_____ (see) beautiful animals and plants. There was an audio connection too – Justin ⁷_____ (talk) about the animals and plants and we ⁸_____ (ask) him questions. It was a great experience.

Posted by Carly

2 Read Carly's answers. Write the questions.

1 No, I didn't go into the water.
2 Yes, I had a great time.
3 No, I didn't take any photos.
4 I went with my friends.

3 >> MB Work in pairs. You were on the boat in the photo. Ask and answer questions with these words.

1 Where / go?   4 Who / talk to?
2 When / arrive?   5 Why / go?
3 What / see?

I CAN	
talk about the past (regular and irregular past simple verbs)	
ask and answer questions about the past (question words)	

Vocabulary

4 Read about David's day. Complete the sentences with eight of these verbs.

cleaned	cut	drove	fell	finished
found	made	met	paid	sent
swam	took			

Yesterday I ¹_____ breakfast. When I ²_____ my room, I ³_____ twenty euros. I ⁴_____ a text to my friend Alex. I ⁵_____ to a café and I ⁶_____ Alex. He ⁷_____ a photo of me. I ⁸_____ for lunch with the twenty euros!

5 >> MB Write true sentences for you with six of the verbs from Exercise 4 and time expressions.

Last night / weekend / week / month / year
On Monday / Tuesday, etc.

6 >> MB Work in pairs. Read your sentences. Did you do the same things?

I CAN	
talk about people's lives	
say when people did things	

Real life

7 Read the conversation between two colleagues. Choose the best option.

A: Did you have ¹*a good day at the beach / a nice meal / a good holiday* last night?
B: No, I didn't.
A: Oh? Why not?
B: The food was delicious, but my friend ²*missed the plane / saw a shark in the sea / cut her hand with her knife*!
A: Oh no!

8 Work in pairs. Practise the conversation in Exercise 7 with the other two options.

I CAN	
talk about the past	
give reasons for events in the past	

Unit 12 The weekend

Friends have lunch in Riyadh, Saudi Arabia.

1 Work in pairs. Look at the photo of friends on their day off work. What days do you work or study?

2 Look at these activities people do at the weekend. Do people do these activities at home (H) or outside the home (O)?

cook a meal for family and friends	go to a concert
	meet friends
get up late	play football
go out for a meal	play video games
go shopping	visit family
go to the cinema	

3 ▶ 180 Listen to three friends. Tick (✓) the activities in Exercise 2 they talk about.

4 Work in pairs. How often do you do the weekend activities in Exercise 2? Is your weekend similar or different to your partner?

I often get up late at the weekend.

Me too.

12a At home

Vocabulary rooms in a house

1 Look at the things (1–5) there are in different rooms. Write the rooms next to the things.

> bathroom   bedroom   dining room
> ~~kitchen~~   living room

1 a cooker, a fridge   *kitchen*
2 a chair, a table   ....
3 an armchair, a sofa   ....
4 a bed, a wardrobe   ....
5 a bath, a shower, a toilet   ....

2 ▶ 181 Listen and check your answers from Exercise 1.

3 ▶ 182 Listen and repeat the words for the rooms.

4 Work in pairs. Tell your partner one thing about each room in your home.

> *We don't have a dining room. We eat in the kitchen.*

> *My kitchen is very small.*

Listening

5 Look at the photos (1–5) of a family at home in Indonesia. Which rooms are the people in?

6 ▶ 183 Match the sentences with the photos. Then listen and check.

a They're washing their motorbikes.
b She's making lunch.
c He's playing a computer game with his son.
d He's bathing his daughter.
e They're drinking coffee.

7 ▶ 183 Listen again and say who the people are. Write the people next to the sentences in Exercise 6.

> *She's making lunch.*

Ayu's mother

HOME LIFE
PHOTO PROJECT

This week our photo project is about the important things in the home. This is Ayu's home and family. It's Saturday morning in her home in Sumatra, Indonesia.

Grammar present continuous

▶ **PRESENT CONTINUOUS**

I	am (not)	talking.
You/We/You/They	are (not)	cooking.
He/She/It	is (not)	making lunch.

Now look at page 180.

8 Look at the grammar box. Then look at the sentences in Exercise 6. Which auxiliary verb do we use to make the present continuous?

9 Complete the sentences about the photos.

1 _Ayu's mother_ is cooking.
2 _____ are smiling.
3 _____ are sitting on the floor.
4 _____ is lying on the sofa.
5 _____ is wearing an orange T-shirt.

10 Look at the photos again and write true sentences. Use the negative form when necessary.

1 Ayu's mother / eat
   Ayu's mother isn't eating.
2 Amir / play with his daughter.
3 Ayu's father and his friend / talk.
4 Amir's brother / watch TV.
5 Ayu's brother and his friend / wash their cars.

▶ **PRESENT CONTINUOUS QUESTIONS and SHORT ANSWERS**

	Am	I	reading?
(What)	Are	you/we/you/they	doing?
	Is	he/she/it	

Yes, **I am**. No, **I'm not**.
Yes, **you/we/you/they are**.
No, **you/we/you/they aren't**.
Yes, **she/he/it is**. No, **she/he/it isn't**.

Now look at page 180.

11 Look at the grammar box. Choose the correct question form (a–c).

a Are you play?
b He is playing?
c Are they playing?

12 Write questions about the photos. Then work in pairs. Ask and answer the questions.

photo 1: she / cook?
photo 2: what / the baby / look at?
photo 3: they / read?
photo 4: what / they / do?
photo 5 : what / they / wash?

13 Work in pairs. Turn to page 157.

Speaking ⟨ my life ⟩

14 Work in groups. Show some photos you have on your phone to the group. Take turns to ask and answer questions.

Who's that?

That's my cousin and her husband.

What are they doing?

They're singing.

12b Next weekend

Reading

1 Look at the information about three events. Complete the table.

	What?	Where?	When?
a		a shop	
b	a talk		
c			

2 Read the messages between two friends, Alex and Lauren. Which event in Exercise 1 do they talk about?

▶ 184

1 Monday

A What are you doing next weekend? Do you want to meet on Saturday?

L Sorry, I can't. I'm meeting my sister on Saturday. We're going for a walk.

A How about Sunday? I'm going to a concert in the City Hall in the evening. Do you want to come?

L OK. Send me the details.

2 Sunday

L What time are we meeting tonight?

A What about 7.30? Is that OK?

L Yes, that's fine. See you outside the City Hall.

Grammar present continuous for the future

▶ **PRESENT CONTINUOUS FOR THE FUTURE**

*What are you doing **next weekend**?*
*I'm going shopping with my sister **on Saturday**.*
*I'm going to a concert **in the evening**.*

Now look at page 180.

3 Look at the grammar box. Are the sentences about now or a time in the future?

4 ▶ 185 Look at the information for the Natural Science Museum in Exercise 1. Write the conversation between two friends. Then listen and check.

1 A: What / you / do / next weekend?
2 B: I'm not sure. My brother / come / tomorrow.
3 A: he / stay the weekend?
4 B: Yes, he is. We / go / for a meal / Saturday evening.
5 A: Helen Smith / give a talk / Sunday afternoon. Do you want to come?
  B: Yes, that's a great idea.

5 Pronunciation *going* and *doing*

a ▶ 186 Listen to four sentences. Notice the /w/ sound in *going* and *doing*.

b ▶ 186 Listen and repeat the sentences. Pay attention to the /w/ sound in *going* and *doing*.

6 Look at the information about people's activities for next weekend. Write true sentences with these words. Use affirmative and negative forms.

1 Aisha / shopping / Sunday morning
   Aisha isn't going shopping on Sunday morning.
2 Aisha / a cake / Saturday afternoon
3 Aisha / tennis / Sunday morning
4 Bernardo / friends / Saturday afternoon
5 Bernardo / TV / Sunday afternoon
6 Che and Dan / walk / Saturday morning
7 Che and Dan / football / Sunday morning.
8 Che and Dan / Che's parents / Sunday afternoon.

		Saturday	Sunday
Aisha	am	go shopping	play tennis
	pm	make a cake	
Bernardo	am	meet friends	
	pm		watch TV
Che and Dan	am	go for a walk	play football
	pm		visit Che's parents

Speaking *my life*

7 Make a diary for next weekend. Write activities for these times.

Saturday

MORNING	
AFTERNOON	
EVENING	

Sunday

MORNING	
AFTERNOON	
EVENING	

8 Work in pairs. Take turns to invite your partner to do activities with you.

> *Do you want to go shopping on Saturday morning?*

> *Sorry, I'm playing football. What about the afternoon?*

Saturday afternoon in a café in Paris

12c A different kind of weekend

Reading

1 Look at the photos on page 147. Answer the questions.

1 What do you think the people are doing?
2 Where do you think they are?
3 Do you think there is anything unusual about them?

2 Read the article *A different kind of weekend* and check your ideas from Exercise 1.

3 Read the article again. Are the sentences true (T) or false (F)?

1 Joel works for free at the weekend.
2 He's building a house for his family.
3 He works with his friends.
4 He's helping different people next weekend.

Grammar prepositions of place (2)

▶ **PREPOSITIONS OF PLACE (2)**

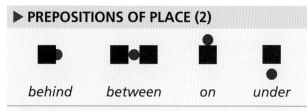

| behind | between | on | under |

Now look at page 180.

4 Look at the grammar box. Read the sentences and look at the photos on page 147. Write S (small photo) or L (large photo).

1 There are five people on the roof.　*L*
2 The house is behind the woman with the green top.
3 The green board is between two blue boards.
4 There's a blue board under the man's hand.

Grammar tense review

▶ **TENSE REVIEW**

1 *Joel Connor works in an office in Kansas.*
2 *The community started a project.*
3 *Joel is working with Jill and Scott Eller.*
4 *Next weekend, Joel is moving to a different project.*

Now look at page 180.

5 Look at the grammar box. <u>Underline</u> the verbs in the sentences (1–4) from the article. Then write past (P), present (PR) or future (F) next to the sentences.

6 Complete the sentences with the correct tense of the verbs.

1 Sam _____ (go) to work every day.
2 Last year, my family _____ (move) to a new house.
3 Next week, we _____ (help) friends in their garden.

7 Match the questions (1–5) with the answers (a–e). Then write past (P), present (PR) or future (F) next to the sentences.

1 What do you do?
2 What are you doing?
3 What do you usually do at the weekend?
4 What did you do at the weekend?
5 What are you doing at the weekend?

a I'm going to a concert with a friend.
b I'm a builder.
c I visited my cousin in London.
d I'm making lunch.
e I meet my friends.

Speaking 〔my life〕

8 Work in groups. Plan a special weekend for a person you all know. Then tell the class.

> *Next weekend is our special weekend for Esther. On Saturday morning, we're all going shopping. After that, ...*

A different kind of weekend

▶ 187

Joel Connor works in an office in Kansas. His job is a typical nine-to-five, Monday-to-Friday job. So at the weekend, he does something different. He helps people for free. Every weekend, there's a new project. This weekend, Joel is helping to build a house. You can see him in the photo. He's moving a large blue board. All the people are 'weekend builders'.

These 'weekend builders' are from the small town of Greensburg in Kansas. A year ago, a tornado hit their town. After the tornado, the community started a project to build new homes. The project is for thirty new homes.

Joel says, 'I heard about the tornado and the new project. I knew some people in Greensburg. I wanted to help.' Joel's working with Jill and Scott Eller. Jill and Scott are building their 'dream house'. They're making the house 'tornado-resistant' – that's why it has an unusual shape.

The Ellers' house is almost ready, so next weekend Joel is moving to a different project. Why does he do this at the weekend? 'I have time, I can help people, I make friends and it's fun! So why not?' he says.

12d Would you like to come?

Vocabulary **times and places**

1 Look at the expressions for times and places. <u>Underline</u> the prepositions.

1 **next** week / month / year / Friday /
....

2 **tomorrow** morning / night /
....

3 **on** the table / ....
4 **on Tuesday** morning / afternoon /
....

5 **in the** morning / afternoon / ....
6 **in** town / ....
7 **at** our house / ....
8 **at** eight o'clock / ....

2 Work in pairs. Add one more time or place to each expression in Exercise 1.

Real life **offers and invitations**

3 ▶ 188 Listen to a conversation between George, Samira and Kris. Answer the questions.

1 Who's moving to a new house?
2 When's he/she moving?
3 What's happening in the old house on Sunday?

4 ▶ 188 Listen to the conversation again. Look at the expressions for OFFERS AND INVITATIONS. Tick (✓) the expressions you hear. Write O (offer) or I (invitation) next to the questions.

> **▶ OFFERS AND INVITATIONS**
>
> Would you like a drink?
> Would you like to come?
> Do you want to come?
> I'd like to come.
> I'd like a cup of tea.
> Sorry, I can't make it.
> Yes, please.

5 Pronunciation *would you … ?*

a ▶ 189 Listen to four questions with *would you like …?* Notice the /dʒ/ sound in *would you*.

b ▶ 189 Listen again and repeat the questions. Pay attention to the /dʒ/ sound.

c Work in pairs. Make offers and invitations with *would you like … ?*

to go to the cinema	a cup of coffee
to play football	a seat
to join us	a glass of water

6 Work in new pairs. Take turns to make offers for each situation. How many offers can you make?

Your partner is …

- cold
- hungry

- thirsty
- tired

Would you like my jacket?

No, thanks.

Would you like a hat?

my life ▶ MY PHOTOS ▶ NEXT WEEKEND ▶ A SPECIAL WEEKEND ▶ OFFERS AND INVITATIONS
▶ A THANK YOU NOTE

12e Thank you!

Writing a thank you note

1 Work in pairs. Look at the photo. What's the problem?

2 Read the note. Then read the pairs of sentences (a–c). Which pair of sentences completes (…) the note to Lili?

> Dear Lili
> Thank you for a fantastic weekend! We had a great time. On the way home, we had a little problem. (See attached photo!) … We're using Dad's car this week – he's taking the train to work. Speak to you soon.
> Best wishes
> Bibia and Mark

a Our plane was late! So we stayed in a hotel for the night.

b We went on the wrong road! We got home at midnight!

c We had a problem with the car! My parents came and helped us.

3 Writing skill spelling: verb endings

a <u>Underline</u> these verbs in the note. Write the infinitives. What's the spelling change?

1 using _____   2 taking _____

b Complete the table. Make sure you spell the verbs correctly.

	Present continuous	Present simple (*he/she/it*)	Past simple
come			
do			
drive			drove
lie			lay
make			made
see			
smile			
study			
swim			swam
travel			

4 Choose one of these sentences. Write a 'thank you' note to the friend for his/her help. Include a sentence with one of the adjectives.

- A friend sent you some photos.
- You had a meal at a friend's house.
- A friend gave you some books.
- You stayed with a friend for the weekend.

> amazing   beautiful   fantastic   great
> interesting   lovely

6 Check your note. Check the past simple verbs.

7 Work in pairs. Exchange notes. Ask a follow-up question about your partner's note.

12f A day in the life of a lighthouse keeper

The lighthouse at Cabo Polonio in Uruguay

Before you watch

1 Look at the photo on page 150. Where do we usually see lighthouses?

2 Complete the text about Cabo Polonio with these words.

> coast   lighthouse   people   road

Cabo Polonio is a small village on the east ¹ _____ of Uruguay. There aren't any roads to Cabo Polonio. It's about seven kilometres to the main ² _____ . There are about 95 ³ _____ in the village and there is a ⁴ _____ . It was built in 1881.

3 Key vocabulary

a Read the sentences. Match the underlined words (1–3) with the pictures (a–c).

1 We eat stew a lot in winter.
2 *Mate* is a popular drink in South America.
3 I use tools a lot in my job.

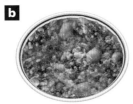

b ▶ 190 Listen and repeat the underlined words.

4 ▶ 191 Look at the word box. Listen and repeat the words.

5 Work in pairs. The person who works in a lighthouse is called a lighthouse keeper. What do you think a lighthouse keeper does every day?

While you watch

6 ☐◀ 12 Complete the activities (a–i) with these words. Then watch the video and tick (✓) the activities you see.

> clothes   a machine   a meal   outside

a checking a light
b cleaning _____
c cleaning stairs
d cooking _____
e cutting meat
f making *mate*
g repairing things
h sitting _____
i washing _____

7 ☐◀ 12 Watch the video again. Put the activities in Exercise 6 in order.

repairing things   1

After you watch

8 Work in pairs. Write the commentary for the video. Follow these steps.

1 Give the lighthouse keeper a name.
2 Describe the weather.
3 Use the vocabulary from Exercise 6 and your own ideas. Write sentences. Use the present simple.
4 Practise reading your commentary. Take turns.

9 What would you like to ask the lighthouse keeper? Write three questions.

10 Work in pairs. Compare your questions and imagine the lighthouse keeper's responses.

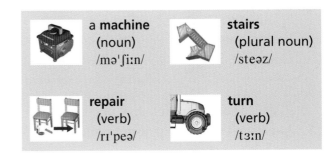

	a machine (noun) /məˈʃiːn/		**stairs** (plural noun) /steəz/
	repair (verb) /rɪˈpeə/		**turn** (verb) /tɜːn/

Grammar

1 Look at the photo of people at a bus stop in Santiago, Chile. Match these words (1–5) with the people (a–e). Then write sentences with the present continuous.

1 make / a phone call
2 wear / a brown jacket
3 hold / some books
4 talk / to her friend
5 walk / to the bus stop

2 Complete the paragraph about the photo with the present continuous.

It's Friday evening in Santiago. These people ¹ _____ (stand) at a bus stop. There's a bus at the bus stop. The bus doors ² _____ (open), but the people ³ _____ (not get) on the bus. They ⁴ _____ (wait) for different buses. Some of the people ⁵ _____ (go) home. They ⁶ _____ (think) about the weekend. Some ⁷ _____ (not go) home – they ⁸ _____ (take) the bus to work.

3 >> MB Work in pairs. Ask and answer questions with the present continuous.

1 you / study / at the moment?
2 where / you / go / tomorrow?
3 you / meet friends / this weekend?
4 what / you / do / on Sunday?

I CAN	
talk about now (present continuous)	
talk about the future (present continuous with future time expressions)	
use the present simple, present continuous and past simple correctly	

Vocabulary

4 >> MB Work in pairs. Where do people do these things? Ask and answer questions about rooms with these words.

1 make meals   4 watch TV
2 sleep   5 eat
3 have a shower   6 read

5 >> MB Work in pairs. Tell your partner about the things you usually do at the weekend. Do you do similar things?

I CAN	
talk about weekend activities	
talk about rooms in a house	

Real life

6 Match the offers and invitations (1–4) with the responses (a–d).

1 Would you like a drink?
2 Are you hungry? How about a sandwich?
3 Do you want to meet on Sunday?
4 Would you like to go to the cinema tomorrow?

a Great. What time is good for you?
b Sorry, I can't make tomorrow.
c Yes, please. Just a glass of water.
d No thanks, I'm fine.

7 Work in pairs. Practise the conversations in Exercise 6. Change the responses.

I CAN	
make and respond to offers and invitations	

UNIT 2b, Exercise 13, page 25
Student A

1 Look at the photo. You are on holiday in Oman. Look at the sentences (1–4) and choose an option. Then have a telephone conversation with your friend (Student B).

1 You're *OK / happy*.
2 It's *hot / cold*.
3 The beach is *nice / beautiful*.
4 Your hotel is *nice / OK*.

2 Your friend (Student B) is on holiday. Prepare questions with these words. Then have a telephone conversation with Student B.

1 where?
2 OK?
3 cold?
4 city / beautiful?
5 hotel / nice?

UNIT 4b, Exercise 8, page 49
Student A

1 Look at the information about photo A. Answer your partner's questions.

The Paranel observatory
• It's in the Atacama desert in Chile.
• It's open on Saturdays.
• It's big.
• It's in the James Bond film *Quantum of Solace*.

2 Look at photo B. Ask your partner the questions in the grammar box on page 49.

UNIT 8b, Exercise 11, page 97
Student A

1 Look at the information. Ask questions about Paulo to complete the table.

Does Paulo watch videos online?

2 Answer your partner's questions about Eva.

3 Complete the information for you.

4 Answer your partner's questions.

5 Ask your partner questions and complete the information for 'your partner'.

Do you watch videos online?

6 Are you or your partner similar to Paulo or Eva?

	Paulo	Eva	You	Your partner
watch videos online?		✗		
go to classes in the evenings?		✓ mornings		
drink coffee?		✓		
do homework at weekends?		✗		
have lunch at home?		✓ at work		
meet friends after class?		✗		

UNIT 9b, Exercise 13, page 109
Student A

Ask your partner about the Sun Hotel. Then look at the information about the Mountain Hotel. Answer your partner's questions. Then decide which of the three hotels you want to stay in.

	Seaview Hotel	Mountain Hotel	Sun Hotel
wi-fi?	✓	✓	
a car park?	✓	✓	
a restaurant?	✓	✗	
rooms with a fridge?	✓	✗	
a swimming pool?	✓	✗	
the city centre?	✗	✓	
price?	$145 a night	$90 a night	$ … a night

UNIT 2b, Exercise 13, page 25
Student B

1 Your friend (Student A) is on holiday. Prepare questions with these words. Then have a telephone conversation with Student A about your holiday.

1 where?
2 OK?
3 cold?
4 beach / beautiful?
5 hotel / nice?

2 Look at the photo. You are on holiday in New York. Look at the sentences (1–4) and choose an option. Then have a telephone conversation with your friend (Student A) about your holiday.

1 You're *OK / happy*.
2 It's *hot / cold*.
3 The city is *nice / beautiful*.
4 Your hotel is *nice / OK*.

UNIT 4b, Exercise 8, page 49
Student B

1 Look at photo A. Ask your partner the questions in the grammar box on page 49.

2 Look at the information about photo B. Answer your partner's questions.

The Taj Mahal
• It's in Agra in India.
• It's open every day except Fridays.
• It's beautiful. It's a UNESCO World Heritage Site.

UNIT 8b, Exercise 10, page 97
Student B

1 Look at the information. Answer your partner's questions about Paulo.

2 Ask questions about Eva to complete the table.

> *Does Eva watch videos online?*

3 Complete the information for you.

4 Ask your partner questions and complete the information for 'your partner'.

> *Do you watch videos online?*

5 Answer your partner's questions.

6 Are you or your partner similar to Paulo or Eva?

	Paulo	Eva	You	Your partner
watch videos online?	✓ on TV			
go to classes in the evenings?	✗			
drink coffee?	✗ tea			
do homework at weekends?	✓			
have lunch at home?	✗			
meet friends after class?	✓			

UNIT 9b, Exercise 13, page 109
Student B

Look at the information about the Sun Hotel. Answer your partner's questions. Then ask about the Mountain Hotel. Then decide which of the three hotels you want to stay in.

	Seaview Hotel	Mountain Hotel	Sun Hotel
wi-fi?	✓		✓
a car park?	✓		✓
a restaurant?	✓		✓
rooms with a fridge?	✓		✓
a swimming pool?	✓		✗
the city centre?	✗		✓
price?	$145 a night	$... a night	$110 a night

UNIT 6c, Exercise 10, page 74

Student A

1 Look at the photos and choose an item. Answer your partner's questions. You can answer *yes* or *no*.

2 Repeat with two or three more food and drink words. Take turns.

Student B

1 Look at the photos. Ask questions to find out your partner's item. You can ask questions with *yes* or *no* answers.

> *Can you have it for breakfast / lunch / dinner?*

> *Can you have it in a restaurant?*

> *Is it a fruit / vegetable / snack?*   *Is it a food / drink?*

> *Is it red / white / brown, etc?*   *Is it hot / cold?*

 avocado

 cereal

 cheese

 lemonade

 milk

orange juice

 pasta

 soup

 yogurt

UNIT 12a, Exercise 13, page 143

Student A

Look at the photo of Ayu's family in the living room. Write questions. Then ask and answer the questions with your partner.

1 children / watch TV?
2 man / sit on a chair?
3 people in the kitchen / talk?

Student B

Look at the photo of Ayu's family in the living room. Write questions. Then ask and answer the questions with your partner.

1 boy / lie on the sofa?
2 girls / sit on the floor?
3 women / wear scarves?

GRAMMAR SUMMARY UNIT 1

be: *I + am, you + are*

I	am ('m)	Simon.
You	are ('re)	Anna.

Contractions
  I'm = I am
  You're = You are

> I'm Simon.

> I'm Anna.

> You're Anna.

> You're Simon.

▶ **Exercises 1 and 2**

be: *he/she/it + is*

He	is ('s)	from São Paulo.
She	is ('s)	Brazilian.
It	is ('s)	in Brazil.

Contractions
  He's = He is
  She's = She is
  It's = It is

He is   She is   It is

▶ **Exercises 3 and 4**

be: *I + am, you + are, he/she/it + is*

I	am ('m)	John.
You	are ('re)	a student.
He	is ('s)	Spanish.
She	is ('s)	from Vietnam.
It	is ('s)	in Italy.

▶ **Exercises 5 and 6**

my, your

I'm Simon. **My** name's Simon.
You're Anna. **Your** name's Anna.

> It's my book.

> It's your book.

> My name's Maya.

> Your name's John.

▶ **Exercise 7**

Exercises

1 Write *I'm* or *You're*.

1 Hello. **I'm** Jack.

Hi. _____ Susana.

2 Hello. _____ your teacher. _____ in my class.

2 Write *I'm* or *You're*.

1 GEORGE: _____ George.
  TERESA: Hi, George.
2 OTTO: _____ Carola.
  CAROLA: Yes!
3 TERESA: Hello.
  OTTO: Hi! _____ Otto Hampel.
4 GEORGE: Hello! _____ George.
  CAROLA: Hi, George.

3 Write *He*, *She* or *It*.

1 *She* 's Italian.

2 _____ 's a chair.

3 _____ 's from Egypt.

4 _____ 's an English book.

5 _____ 's American.

6 _____ 's from Mexico.

4 Write sentences with *He's*, *She's* and *It's*.

1 Jack / from London
  He's from London.
2 George / Canadian
  _____
3 Katya / Russian
  _____
4 Chicago / in the United States
  _____
5 Jessica / from Toronto
  _____
6 Cairo / in Egypt
  _____

5 Write *am*, *are* and *is*.

1 Hi! I _____ Elena.
2 Paul _____ a doctor.
3 He _____ from Hong Kong.
4 It _____ in China.
5 You _____ English.
6 I _____ Mexican.

6 Put the words in order to make sentences. Write sentences with contractions if possible.

1 is / the United Kingdom / it / from
  It's from the United Kingdom.
2 Mexico / is / Elisabeth / from
  _____
3 from / are / you / Vietnam
  _____
4 Spanish / is / the teacher
  _____
5 is / Brazilian / he
  _____
6 in / New York / am / I
  _____

7 Complete the sentences with *my* and *your*.

1 _____ name's Ludmilla. I'm from Russia.
2 Hello! I'm Tomas. You're my teacher. _____ name's Mr Jones.
3 Hello! _____ name's Paolo.
4 Hi. I'm Juan. What's _____ name?
5 A: _____ mobile number is 695 836 736.
  B: Thanks.
6 A: Ben, what's _____ home number?
  B: It's 0352 497 268.

be: we/they + are

We	are ('re)	in Canada.
They	are ('re)	on a beach.
		doctors.

Contractions
    We're = We are
    They're = They are

We're on a beach.

They're doctors.

▶ Exercises 1 and 2

be: negative forms

I	am not ('m not)	a teacher.
You	are not (aren't)	from Italy.
He/She/It	is not (isn't)	on a beach.
We/You/They	are not (aren't)	from Italy.
		on a beach.

Contractions
    aren't = are not
    isn't = is not

▶ Exercise 3

be: questions and short answers

Questions	
Are you	in a hotel?
Is he/she/it	cold?
Are we/you/they	from London?
Short answers	
Yes, I am. / No, I'm not.	
Yes, he/she/it is. / No, he/she/it isn't.	
Yes, we/you/they are. / No, we/you/they aren't.	

Affirmative form → Question form
    It's cold.   →   **Is it** cold?
    it is   →   is it

Short answers

Yes, I am. ✓   Yes, I'm. ✗
Yes, he/she/it is. ✓   Yes, he's / she's / it's. ✗
Yes, we/you/they are. ✓   Yes, we're / you're / they're. ✗

▶ Exercises 4 and 5

a/an

a book, a city
an animal, an island

a/an = one thing

a + single noun with consonants: b, c, d, f, etc.
an + single noun with vowels: a, e, i, o, u

EDUCATION CONFERENCE
Josh Lees LONDON 10-14 May

a phone   an ID card

▶ Exercise 6

Plural nouns

books, cities, beaches

Spelling changes
Add -s.
    a car   →   cars
    airport, door, lake, photo, student, table, etc.
Change y to ies.
    a country   →   countries
Add -es to nouns that end in -s, -ch and -ss.
    a bus   →   buses
    a car   →   cars ✓ a cars ✗

Television   International
Marina BRUNETTI
VISITOR   12/14/2018
EDUCATION CONFERENCE
Josh Lees LONDON 10-14 May

phones   ID cards

▶ Exercise 7

Exercises

1 Complete the sentences with *We* or *They*.

1 _____'re in Paris.

2 _____'re taxis.

3 _____'re in London.

4 _____'re Spanish.

2 Complete the sentences.

1 This is Jack. This is Bill. *They* are Canadian.
2 France and Spain _____ in Europe.
3 Bruno and Paola are from Italy. _____ Italian.
4 I'm with my teacher. _____'re in a classroom.
5 I'm from Japan. My friend is from Japan. _____ Japanese.
6 Jane and Barry are Australian. _____'re from Australia.

3 Rewrite the sentences with the verb in the negative form.

1 Jack's a student.
   Jack isn't a student.
2 We are Spanish.

3 The city is in Europe.

4 I'm happy.

5 Susana and Gina are from Tunisia.

6 You're a teacher.

4 Rewrite the sentences as questions.

1 Sydney is in Australia.
   Is Sydney in Australia?
2 You're from Egypt.

3 London is cold.

4 We're in a hotel.

5 Katya is an artist.

6 They're doctors.

5 Write questions with the correct form of *be*. Then write two answers for each question with *yes* and *no*.

1 Simon / from Bolivia?
   Is Simon from Bolivia?
   Yes, he is.   No, he isn't.
2 you / on holiday?

3 your hotel / nice?

4 Susana and Gina / in Paris?

6 Write *a or an*.

1 I'm _a_ student.
2 Sonia is _____ doctor.
3 Malta is _____ island in the Mediterranean Sea.
4 This is _____ book.
5 You aren't _____ teacher.
6 Is this _____ animal?

7 Write the plural of these nouns.

1 a lake _____
2 a country _____
3 a beach _____
4 a holiday _____
5 an island _____
6 an address _____
7 a photo _____
8 a boat _____

his, her, its, our, their

What's	my your his her its our their	name?

Her book.

Her books.

Their book.

Their books.

What's his name?

This is my school. Its name is London Languages.

This is our house.

Their children are in my class.

▶ **Exercises 1 and 2**

Possessive 's

This is **Oscar's** car.
Jack's eyes are brown.

The possessive 's is not a contraction of *is*.
Who's Jack? = Who is Jack?
He's my brother. = He is my brother.
He's Maria's son. = He is Maria's son.

Oscar's car

Raul's phones

Maria's children

Fatima's cats

▶ **Exercises 3, 4 and 5**

Irregular plural nouns

a child	→	**children**
a man	→	**men**
a woman	→	**women**
a person	→	**people**

children

men

women

people

a child → children ✓ ~~a children~~ ✗

Add -s or -es and change -y to -ies to make regular plural nouns.

▶ **Exercise 6**

Exercises

1 Choose the correct option.

1 This is a photo of my brother in ~~her~~ / *his* car.
2 My husband is Russian. *His* / *My* name is Boris.
3 We are happy. It's *his* / *our* daughter's wedding.
4 Hi, Zara. Is this *her* / *your* mother?
5 My friends are in Spain. It's *his* / *their* holiday.
6 My friend's name is Anya. *Her* / *Your* husband's name is Bruno.

2 Complete the sentences with these words.

> he   her   his   it   its   she   their
> they

1 A: Robert's address is 25 London Road.
  B: What's ___*his*___ phone number?'
2 A: Dani and Harry are brothers.
  B: What's _____ surname?
3 Sonia is my friend. _____'s a teacher.
4 A: What's your name?
  B: _____'s Paulo.
5 A: My son's called Riz.
  B: How old is _____ ?
6 We're from an island. _____ name is Skye.
7 Venus and Serena are tennis players. Are _____ sisters?
8 Look at Anna in _____ car.

3 Write sentences.

1 James / Oscar / father
  James is Oscar's father.
2 John and James / Elena / sons

3 Lisa and Marga / John / daughters

4 Lisa / Marga / sister

5 James / Harry / son

6 James / John / brother

4 Put the words in order. Write sentences with the possessive 's.

1 hair / Carlo / is / black
  Carlo's hair is black.
2 bag / old / Joana / is

3 car / the teacher / is / new

4 blue / are / eyes / Frieda

5 they / children / Nam / are

6 Michael and David / friends / are / Kim

5 Write *is* or *'s* in the correct place.

1 Who this?
  Who's this?
2 My hair black.

3 How old your best friend?

4 David friends are Oscar and Paul.

5 Sandra tall.

6 Our teacher name is Andrew.

6 Complete the singular and plural nouns.

1 How old are the wom_____ in the photo?
2 Who are the pe_____ at the wedding?
3 This chil_____ is three years old.
4 Who is the pe_____ in your car?
5 James and Eliza are my chil_____.
6 Our teacher is a m_____.

Prepositions of place (1)

The market is **in** London Street.

 The museum is **next to** the market.

The café is **opposite** the bus station.

The cinema is **near** the bank.

▸ **Exercises 1 and 2**

this, that, these, those

This is my book.
That's your book.
These are my books.
Those are your books.

this/that = singular
these/those = plural

Use *this / these* for things near to you.
Use *that / those* for things not near to you.

That is
his pen.

This is
my pen.

These are photos of my holiday.

▸ **Exercises 3 and 4**

Question words

What is that?
Where are the maps?
When is the park open?
Why is Big Ben famous?

Word order in questions with question
words = question word + *be* + subject

Affirmative form	→	Question form
It's famous.	→	**Why is it** famous?
it is	→	is it
The maps are on the table.	→	Where are the maps?
The maps are	→	are the maps

Contractions

What is	→	What's
		What's that? ✓
		~~What's it?~~ ✗
Where is	→	Where's
		Where's the car?
When is	→	When's
		When's it open?
Why is	→	Why's
		Why's it popular?

▸ **Exercise 5**

Are those
your bags?

Exercises

1 Look at the picture of Oxford Street opposite. Write *yes* or *no*.

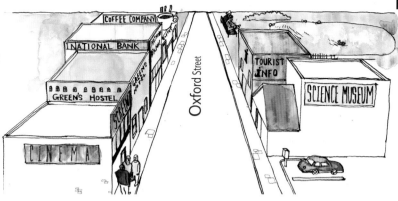

1 Is the cinema next to the bank?
   no

2 Is the park in Oxford Street?

3 Is the Science Museum opposite the cinema?

4 Are the people near the park?

5 Is the café next to the park?

6 Is the Tourist Information Centre opposite the bank?

2 Look at the picture of Oxford Street. Complete the sentences.

1 The bank is ___*next to*___ the hotel.
2 The bank is _____ the Tourist Information Centre.
3 Two people are _____ the park.
4 The car park is _____ the hotel.
5 The Science Museum is _____ the car park.
6 Three people are _____ Oxford Street.

3 Look at the picture of Oxford Street. Read the words of the people in the park (1–3) and of the people in the street (4–6). Choose the correct option.

1 '*This* / *That* park is nice'
2 '*This* / *That* is my bank.'
3 'Is *this* / *that* cinema open?'
4 'Is *this* / *that* Oxford Street?'
5 '*This* / *That* is a beautiful park.'
6 'Is *this* / *that* your car in the car park?'

4 Choose the correct option.

1 Are *these* / ~~those~~ your keys?

2 *These* / *Those* buildings are old.

3 Are *these* / *those* dictionaries?

4 *These* / *Those* are my children.

5 *These* / *Those* aren't maps of London.

6 Are *these* / *those* lions?

5 Put the words in order to make questions.

1 is / building / what / that / ?
   What is that building?

2 is / open / the museum / when / ?

3 your friends / are / where / today / ?

4 is / why / the café / popular / ?

5 to London / are / when / the buses / ?

can/can't

Affirmative	
I/You He/She/It We/You/They	**can** cook.
Negative	
I/You He/She/It We/You/They	**can't** cook.

Contractions
  can't = cannot

▶ **Exercise 1**

can questions and short answers

Questions		
Can	I/you he/she/it we/you/they	cook?
Short answers		
Yes, No,	I/you he/she/it we/you/they	**can.** **can't.**

Word order in questions with *can* = can + subject + verb

Affirmative form	→	Question form
She can drive.	→	*Can she drive?*
she can	→	*can she*

can = ability   *can* = request

I can speak English.

Can I have two coffees, please?

▶ **Exercises 2 and 3**

have/has

I/You We/You/They	**have**	a car. two guitars.
He/She/It	**has**	

We have a car.

Mr and Mrs Smith have three children.

The house has a blue door.

Susana has two guitars.

▶ **Exercise 4**

be + adjective

My car is **old.**
Your children are **beautiful.**
His camera isn't **new.**
Are these glasses **expensive**?

The adjective is the same with singular and plural subjects.
    The car is expensive.
    The glasses are expensive. ✓ ~~expensives.~~ ✗

▶ **Exercise 5**

Adjective + noun

The **car** is **blue.**	→	It's a **blue car.**
The **photos** are **big.**	→	They're **big photos.**

Word order = adjective + noun, NOT noun + adjective
    I have new glasses. ✓
    I have ~~glasses new.~~ ✗

▶ **Exercise 6**

Exercises

1 Choose the correct option.

1 Babies *can / can't* run.
2 Children *can / can't* see.
3 Babies *can / can't* move.
4 Cars *can / can't* fly.
5 Children *can / can't* run.
6 Animals *can / can't* speak.

2 Put the words in order to make sentences and questions.

1 play / piano / you / can / the / ?
   Can you play the piano?
2 car / drive / can't / I / a / .

3 friends / my / cook / can't / .

4 baby / walk / your / can / ?

5 can't / robot / swim / this / .

6 speak / my / Russian / can / brother / .

3 Write questions and answers.

1 he / sing ✓
   Can he sing?
   Yes, he can.
2 you / drive a car ✓

3 they / play table tennis ✗

4 she / cook ✗

5 we / speak English ✓

6 it / swim ✗

4 Complete the sentences with *have* or *has*.

1 I   *have*   two cameras.
2 My brother _____ a mountain bike.
3 My friends _____ four children –
   they're all boys.
4 We _____ a piano.
5 My city _____ three parks.
6 My sister _____ a job. She's a teacher.

5 Write at least eight sentences with these words and *be*.

The buildings	expensive
My camera	new
Your car	popular
The museum	red
The people	tall
My sister	young

   The buildings are tall.

6 Put the words in order to make sentences.

1 is / camera / this / Japanese / a
   This is a Japanese camera.
2 fantastic / phone / my / a / memory / has

3 MP3 player / you / great / on / your / music / have

4 city / Venice / beautiful / a / is

5 blue / a / my / has / sister / car

6 is / Jack's / man / an / grandfather / old

like

Affirmative	
I You We You They	**like** basketball.
Negative	
I You We You They	**don't like** cycling.

Contractions
don't = do not

Use the verb *do* with *like* to form negatives.

Affirmative form → Negative form
They like swimming. → *They don't like swimming.*

▸ Exercise 1

like questions and short answers

Questions	
Do I **Do** you **Do** we **Do** you **Do** they	**like** sport?
Short answers	
Yes, I/you/we/you/they **do**.	
No, I/you/we/you/they **don't**.	

Use *do* with *like* to form questions.

Affirmative form → Question form
They like sport. → *Do they like sport?*

Short answers
Yes, I do. ✓   Yes, I ~~like~~. ✗
No, I don't. ✓   No, I ~~don't like~~. ✗

▸ Exercises 2 and 3

he/she + like

Affirmative	
He She	**likes** books.
Negative	
He She	**doesn't like** music.

Contractions
doesn't = does not

Questions		
Does	he she	**like** fish?
Short answers		
Yes, he/she **does**.		
No, he/she **doesn't**.		

Use *do* with *like* to form negatives and questions.
He doesn't like TV.
Does she like animals?

Short answers
Yes, he does. ✓   Yes, ~~he likes~~.
                            Yes, he ~~does like~~. ✗
No, she doesn't. ✓   No, she ~~doesn't like~~. ✗

▸ Exercises 4 and 5

Object pronouns

Diana likes	**me**. **you**. **him**. **her**. **it**. **us**. **you**. **them**.

Subject pronouns are before the verb.
I/you/he/she/it/we/you/they like Diana.

Object pronouns are after the verb.
Diana likes me/you/him/her/it/us/you/them.

▸ Exercise 6

Exercises

1 Write sentences with the correct form of *like*.

1 I / basketball ☹
  I don't like basketball.
2 we / rugby ☺

3 they / tennis ☺

4 you / swimming ☹

5 I / London ☺

6 they / coffee ☹

2 Write questions with the words. Then write answers to the questions.

1 Formula 1 / they ✓
  Do they like Formula 1?
  Yes, they do.
2 football / you ✗

3 animals / you ✓

4 the beach / they ✗

3 Rewrite the sentences in the form given in brackets.

1 I like motorbikes. (negative)
  I don't like motorbikes.
2 Your friends like cats. (question)

3 You don't like cities. (affirmative)

4 We don't like running. (affirmative)

5 We like football. (negative)

6 You like bananas. (question)

4 Write sentences with the correct form of *like*.

1 Toni / music ☺
  Toni likes music.
2 Ahmed / detective stories ☹

3 Elena / animals ☺

4 Kim / cold places ☹

5 Tanya / beaches ☺

6 Nuno / fish ☹

5 Four of these sentences have a missing word: *does* or *doesn't*. Rewrite the sentences with the missing word.

1 Nam likes New York.

2 Joanna like films.

3 your teacher like music?

4 Stefan like swimming.

5 Elise like sports?

6 Krishnan likes wildlife shows.

6 Look at the underlined nouns. Complete the sentences with an object pronoun.

1 I like wildlife shows, but my friend doesn't like   *them* .
2 We can't see you. Can you see _____ ?
3 She's a popular writer, but I don't like
   _____ .
4 A: Do you like pop music?
   B: Yes, I love _____ .
5 Matt Damon is fantastic in the *Bourne* films. I love _____ .
6 I have a cat. It loves _____ .

Present simple *I/you/we/you/they*

Affirmative		
I You We You They	**get up**	at six o'clock.
Negative		
I You We You They	**don't get up**	at six o'clock.

Contractions
   don't = do not

Use the verb *do* with the present simple to form negatives.

   Affirmative form → Negative form
   They speak English. → *They don't speak English.*

Use the present simple to talk about routines.
   We watch TV in the evening.

Use the present simple to talk about true things.
   I have two children.

▸ **Exercises 1 and 2**

Prepositions of time

at six o'clock

in the evening

on Monday/Mondays

at night

▸ **Exercise 3**

Present simple questions *I/you/we/you/they*

Questions			
Do	I you we you they	**play** tennis?	
Short answers			

Yes, *I/you/we/you/they* **do**.
No, *I/you/we/you/they* **don't**.

Use *do* with the present simple to form questions.

   Affirmative form → Question form
   They live in London. → *Do they live in London?* ✓
   ~~They live in London?~~ ✗

Short answers
   Yes, they do. ✓   Yes, they ~~live~~. ✗
   No, they don't. ✓   No, they ~~don't live~~. ✗

▸ **Exercises 4 and 5**

Present simple *Wh-* questions

What Where Who Why When	**do**	*I/you/we/you/they*	**do**? **go**? **meet**?

Word order in present simple *Wh-* questions
= *Wh-* word + *do* + subject + verb

Present simple questions and *Wh-* questions:
Affirmative =   *They work.*
Question =   *Do*   *they work?*
Wh- question = *Where*   *do*   *they work?*

▸ **Exercise 6**

Exercises

1 Rewrite the sentences in the form given in brackets.

1 I have breakfast at seven o'clock. (negative)
   I don't have breakfast at seven o'clock.
2 You don't watch TV in the evening. (affirmative)

3 My friends start work at nine o'clock. (negative)

4 I don't have classes on Fridays. (affirmative)

5 We finish class at eight o'clock. (negative)

6 They go to bed at midnight. (negative)

2 Write sentences with these verbs.

not eat	not go	not get up	have
study	~~watch~~		

1 I / TV
   I watch TV.
2 we / to school

3 you / English

4 they / lunch in a café

5 my friends / meat

6 I / at eight o'clock

3 Choose the correct preposition.

1 We don't go to class *at / on* Saturdays and Sundays.
2 They eat cereal *in / on* the morning.
3 I don't drink coffee *at / in* the evening.
4 I finish work *at / in* seven o'clock.
5 You sleep *at / in* night.
6 We get up *at / on* six o'clock.

4 Write questions with the words. Then write answers to the questions.

1 every week (you / dress up) ✓
   Do you dress up every week?
   Yes, we do.
2 football (they / play) ✗

3 cakes (you / make) ✓

4 in a band (your friends / sing) ✓

5 shopping (we / enjoy) ✓

6 photos (you / take) ✗

5 Write sentences and questions with the words in brackets.

1 you / painting / ? (like)
   Do you like painting?
2 My friends / German (not / speak)

3 you / to music / ? (listen)

4 We / the guitar (not / play)

5 I / dinner every evening (cook)

6 Put the words in order to make questions.

1 to the beach / do / go / when / you / ?
   When do you go to the beach?
2 do / they / what / at the beach / do / ?

3 with / do / you / who / sing / ?

4 go / swimming / where / they / do / ?

5 you / go / why / do / running / ?

6 in the evening / you / what / do / do / ?

GRAMMAR SUMMARY UNIT 8

Present simple *he/she/it*

Affirmative		
He She	**drives**	a train.
It	**opens**	at ten o'clock.
Negative		
He She	**doesn't drive**	a bus.
It	**doesn't open**	at nine o'clock.

Contractions
  doesn't = does not

Spelling changes
Add *-s* to the infinitive of the verb.
  drive → *drives*

Add *-es* to verbs that end in *-ch* and *-sh.*
  teach → *teaches*
  finish → *finishes*

The verbs *do, go* and *have* are irregular.
  do → *does*
  go → *goes*
  have → *has*

He drives a train.

It doesn't open at nine o'clock.

▶ **Exercises 1, 2 and 3**

Present simple questions *he/she/it*

Questions		
Does	he she it	**teach?** **work?**
Short answers		

Yes, he/she/it **does.**
No, he/she/it **doesn't.**

wh- questions			
What **Where**	**does**	he she it	**do?** **go?**

Use *does* with the present simple with *he/ she/it* to form questions.

Affirmative form → Question form
She works in a park. → *Does she work in a park?* ✓

Short answers
  Yes, she does. ✓   *Yes, she ~~works~~.* ✗
  No, she doesn't. ✓   *No, she ~~doesn't work~~.* ✗

▶ **Exercises 4 and 5**

Frequency adverbs

0%
  *My friend **never** writes emails.*
  *I **sometimes** travel in my job.*
  *My friend **often** works late.*
  *We **usually** get up early.*
  *I **always** have breakfast.*
100%

Word order with frequency adverbs:
adverb + verb
  He often watches TV.

be + adverb
  I am often late. ✓ *I ~~often am~~ late.* ✗

Use *never* with affirmative verbs.
  She never gets up early. ✓
  She ~~never doesn't get up~~ early. ✗

▶ **Exercise 6**

Exercises

1 Complete the sentences with the correct form of the verbs in brackets.

1 Jack ___works___ (work) in a hospital.
2 Ryan _____ (serve) customers in a café.
3 The bus _____ (not / stop) near my house.
4 Amy _____ (help) people in her job.
5 This button _____ (open) the doors.
6 Kristen _____ (not / walk) to work every day.

2 Complete the text with the correct form of these verbs.

buy	get	go	have	play	sell
use	watch	~~work~~	not / work		

Alain Bofill [1] ___works___ in the city. He
[2] _____ a computer all day. He
[3] _____ and [4] _____ money –
dollars, pounds, euros, etc. He [5] _____
home on the Tube. He [6] _____
home at nine o'clock in the evening. He
[7] _____ dinner and he [8] _____
TV with his family. He [9] _____ on
Saturdays – he [10] _____ golf with his
friends.

3 Rewrite the sentences in the form given in brackets.

1 Your friend live near a beach. (negative)
   Your friend doesn't live near a beach.
2 Ahmed doesn't drive to work. (affirmative)

3 My sister enjoys her job. (negative)

4 The office opens on Sundays. (negative)

5 He doesn't watch videos at work. (affirmative)

6 My friend speaks English. (negative)

4 Write questions with the words in brackets.

1 Simon / Arabic? (understand)
   Does Simon understand Arabic?
2 Anne / German? (speak)

3 Lin / near you? (live)

4 Boris / in the evening? (study)

5 Joana / to university? (go)

6 your friend / English? (teach)

5 Read the sentences. Then write questions with the words in brackets.

1 Carl doesn't finish work at eight o'clock. (nine o'clock ?)
   Does he finish work at nine o'clock?
2 Jon doesn't work in an office. (where ?)

3 Julia doesn't goes to bed late. (early ?)

4 My sister doesn't telephone me at 6.30. (what time ?)

5 My brother doesn't read novels. (what ?)

6 My sister doesn't like tea. (coffee ?)

6 Put the words in order to make sentences.

1 coffee / have / usually / I

2 travels / colleague / my / in her job / often

3 homework / never / our / gives / teacher / us

4 studies / my / at home / friend / sometimes

5 always / I / at night / read

6 my / brother / late / always / works

there is/are

Singular
There's a book in my bag.
There's a camera on my phone.

Plural
There are some books in my bag.
There are two computers in my office.

Contractions

there's = there is

There's a camera on my phone.
= My phone has a camera.

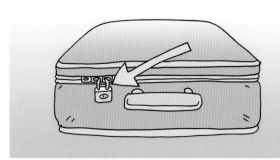

There's a lock on the suitcase.

There's a virus on my computer!

There are some tables near the window.

There are twenty houses in my street.

▸ **Exercises 1 and 2**

there is/are negative and question forms

Negative singular
There isn't a fridge in the room.

Negative plural
There aren't any hotels here.

Contractions

there isn't = there is not
there aren't = there are not

There isn't a fridge in the room.
= The room doesn't have a fridge.

Use *a* after *there isn't*. Use *any* after *there aren't*.

Singular question forms	
Is there a sofa?	Yes, **there is**.
	No, **there isn't**.

Plural question forms	
Are there any trains today?	Yes, **there are**.
	No, **there aren't**.

Affirmative form	→	Question form
There's a sofa.	→	*Is there a sofa?*
there is	→	*is there*
There are some books.	→	*Are there any books?*
there are	→	*are there*

Use *a* after *Is there?* Use *any* after *Are there?*

short answers

Yes, there is. ✓   *Yes, ~~there's~~.* ✗

▸ **Exercises 3, 4 and 5**

Imperative forms

Buy your tickets online.
Don't travel by train.

Contractions

don't = do not

The imperative is the infinitive form of the verb. The negative is *don't* + infinitive.

Imperatives are the same when you speak to one person or more than one person.

▸ **Exercise 6**

Exercises

1 Write *a* or *some* in the correct place.

1 There are pens in my bag.
   There are some pens in my bag.
2 There's tablet on my desk.

3 There are shirts in my suitcase.

4 There are people on this plane.

5 There's scarf in my hand.

6 There's pair of shoes near the door.

2 Look at the picture. Write sentences with the words.

1 a map
   There's a map.
2 keys

3 books

4 a camera

5 a passport

6 clothes

3 Write questions with the words. Then look at the picture in Exercise 2 again and write answers to the questions.

1 a map
   Is there a map?   Yes, there is.
2 a phone

3 pens

4 a passport

5 keys

6 tickets

4 Complete the conversation with the correct forms of *there is / are*.

A: Let's go to Loch Ness for New Year.
B: ¹ _____ an airport near Loch Ness?
A: Yes, ² _____ .
B: ³ _____ flights every day from here?
A: ⁴ _____ flights Monday to Friday, but ⁵ _____ any flights at the weekend.
B: OK. Good idea. Let's go there.

5 Write *a* or *any* in the correct place.

1 Are there chairs in the room?
   Are there any chairs in the room?
2 There aren't bottles in the fridge.

3 Is there shower in the hotel room?

4 There isn't train station in this town.

5 Are there cafés near here?

6 Read the instructions from a travel guide for some tourists. Choose the best option.

1 *Don't forget / Forget* your passports.
2 *Don't arrive / Arrive* at the airport on time.
3 *Don't give / Give* me your mobile numbers, please.
4 *Don't be / Be* late.
5 *Don't wait / Wait* a moment, please.

be: *was/were*

Affirmative		
I/He/She/It	**was**	Russian.
You/We/You/They	**were**	

Use *was* and *were* to talk about the past.

   is → *was*
   are → *were*

Edurne is an explorer.
She was born in 1973.

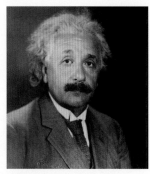

Albert Einstein was German.

The Beatles were English.

▶ **Exercises 1 and 2**

be: *was/were* negative and question forms

Negative		
I/He/She/It	**wasn't**	famous.
You/We/You/They	**weren't**	

Contractions
   wasn't = was not
   weren't = were not

Questions		
Was	I/he/she/it	happy?
Were	you/we/you/they	on TV?

Short answers
Yes, I/he/she/it **was**.
No, I/he/she/it **wasn't**.
Yes, you/we/you/they **were**.
No, you/we/you/they **weren't**.

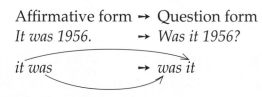

Affirmative form → Question form
It was 1956.   → *Was it 1956?*

  it was   → *was it*

▶ **Exercises 3, 4 and 5**

Regular past simple verbs

Affirmative	
I You He She It We You They	**lived** *from 1480 to 1521.*

Use the past simple to talk about the past.
   Magellan was an explorer. He lived from 1480 to 1521.

Regular past simple verbs end in *-ed*. The form is the same for *I, you, he*, etc.
   live   →   *lived*

Some regular past simple verbs are:

checked	*opened*	*used*
closed	*started*	*visited*
enjoyed	*studied*	*walked*
finished	*travelled*	*watched*
liked	*tried*	*worked*

Spelling changes
Add *-ed* to the infinitive.
   start   → *started*
   watch → *watched*
Add *-d*.
   live   → *lived*
   use   → *used*
Change *-y* after a consonant to *-ied*.
   study → *studied*

▶ **Exercise 6**

Exercises

1 Put the words in order to make sentences.

1 was / the first / Neil Armstrong / on the moon / person
   Neil Armstrong was the first person on the moon.

2 was / Ayrton Senna / racing driver / a

3 parents / born / my / in Zurich / were

4 writer / an / was / Beatrix Potter / English

5 and Magellan / Drake / leaders / were / expedition

6 musician / a / John Lennon / was

2 Complete the paragraph with *was* or *were*.

Sally Ride ¹_____ the first American woman in space. She ²_____ born in 1951. Her parents ³_____ from California. Her first space flight ⁴_____ in 1983. She ⁵_____ the writer of five books for children. They ⁶_____ about space and science.

3 Rewrite the sentences in the form given in brackets.

1 Joe's favourite teacher was Mr Lee. (question)
   Was Joe's favourite teacher Mr Lee?

2 I wasn't at home yesterday. (affirmative)

3 Tran's parents weren't TV presenters. (question)

4 Was your grandmother an important person in your life? (affirmative)

5 David Attenborough's TV shows were about sport. (negative)

6 Were you a good student at school? (negative)

4 Complete the sentences with *was*, *wasn't*, *were* and *weren't*.

1 A: _____ *Sesame Street* your favourite TV show?
   A: No, it _____. It _____ *Friends*.

2 A: Who _____ your best friends at school?
   A: They _____ Angela and Lia.

3 My mother _____ the first woman in her family with a university degree.

4 A: _____ your teachers at school nice?
   A: Yes, they _____.

5 A: _____ the first Olympic Games in Athens?
   A: No, they _____. They _____ in Olympia.

6 I _____ good at music at school and I can't play a musical instrument.

5 Read the sentences. Then write questions with the words in brackets.

1 John Lennon wasn't born in Manchester. (Where ?)
   Where was John Lennon born?

2 Victoria wasn't the first British queen. (Who ?)

3 Sal's sister wasn't born in 2001. (When ?)

4 Nina's grandparents weren't from Hong Kong. (Where ?)

5 Olga's uncle was famous. (Why ?)

6 Teo's parents weren't born in Europe. (Where ?)

6 Write the past simple form of the verbs.

1 My grandfather *died* (die) in 2006.
2 I _____ (live) in Rome from 2014 to 2017.
3 My mother _____ (study) science at university.
4 James _____ (work) in a café in 2016.
5 We _____ (visit) Florida last summer.
6 My friend and I _____ (watch) a good film on Saturday.

Irregular past simple verbs

Affirmative	
I/You He/She/It We/You/They	**went** to the Alps. **had** a good holiday.

Use the past simple to talk about the past.

Irregular past simple verbs have the same form for *I, you, he*, etc.

be	→	*was/were*	*have* → *had*
buy	→	*bought*	*leave* → *left*
come	→	*came*	*make* → *made*
do	→	*did*	*see* → *saw*
drive	→	*drove*	*speak* → *spoke*
eat	→	*ate*	*take* → *took*
find	→	*found*	*write* → *wrote*
go	→	*went*	

In 2013 ...

We went to Thailand.

In 2014 ...

We saw the Pyramids.

In 2015 ...

We ate pizza in Naples.

In 2016 ...

We bought a house.

In 2017 ...

We had a baby.

▶ **Exercises 1, 2 and 3**

Past simple negative and question forms

Negative	
I/You He/She/It We/You/They	**didn't visit** Paris last summer. **didn't go** on holiday last year.

Questions		
Did	I/you he/she/it we/you/they	**visit** Paris last summer? **go** on holiday last year?

Short answers
Yes, I/you/he/she/it/we/you/they **did**. No, I/you/he/she/it/we/you/they **didn't**.

Contractions
  didn't = did not

Use the past simple of *do* (*did*) + infinitive in past simple negative and question forms.

  We watched TV → We didn't watch TV
  last night.   last night. ✓
  We ~~didn't watched~~ TV last night. ✗
  Did you watch TV last night? ✓
  Did ~~you watched~~ TV last night? ✗

▶ **Exercises 4 and 5**

Past simple *Wh-* questions

Wh- questions			
What			**do?**
Where		I/you	**go?**
When	**did**	he/she/it	**leave?**
Why		we/you/they	**stop?**
Who			**see?**

Word order in past simple *Wh-* questions
= *Wh-* word + *did* + subject + verb

Past simple questions and *Wh-* questions:

Affirmative =			They stopped.
Question =		Did	they stop?
Wh- question =	Why	did	they stop?

▶ **Exercise 6**

Exercises

1 Complete the sentences with the past simple form of the verbs.

1 We _took_ (take) a lot of photos on our holiday.
2 The tourists _____ (go) to all the popular places.
3 I _____ (have) lunch with my friends yesterday.
4 We _____ (see) a great film last week.
5 I _____ (make) dinner for my family last night.
6 My father _____ (leave) school when he was fourteen.

2 Write sentences about things that happened yesterday with the past simple form of the verbs.

buy	come	drive	make	speak
write				

1 my friends / to my house
My friends came to my house.
2 Jean / a lot of emails
_____
3 I / lunch
_____
4 we / to the shops
_____
5 my parents / their plane tickets
_____
6 I / to my sister on Skype
_____

3 Complete the text with the past simple form of the verbs.

Last weekend, we ¹ _____ (go) for a walk in the mountains. We ² _____ (start) early in the morning. We ³ _____ (walk) for two hours. Then we ⁴ _____ (have) a snack. We ⁵ _____ (find) a bag on the walk. We ⁶ _____ (finish) our walk and we ⁷ _____ (take) the bag to the police station. The police ⁸ _____ (find) a lot of money in the bag.

4 Rewrite the sentences in the form given in brackets.

1 I didn't go to university. (affirmative)
I went to university.
2 We ate burgers yesterday. (negative)
_____
3 Shakespeare wrote lots of plays. (question)
_____
4 My friend didn't come to school last week. (question)
_____
5 I lived with my grandparents when I was a child. (negative)
_____
6 Tony didn't meet his wife at work. (affirmative)
_____

5 Complete the interview with a travel writer.

Q: ¹ _____ (you / travel) a lot last year?
A: Yes, I ² _____ . I went to three continents.
Q: Wow! ³ _____ (you / go) to South America?
A: Yes, I did. I went with a friend. We visited Ecuador, Peru and Chile, but we ⁴ _____ (not / have) time to go to Argentina.
Q: ⁵ _____ (you / write) a book about your trip?
A: No, I ⁶ _____ , but I wrote a blog and I made some videos about it.

6 Write Wh - questions for these answers. Use the correct form of the underlined verbs.

1 We met lots of interesting people.
Who did you meet?
2 They went to Cancun in Mexico.
_____
3 She saw some beautiful buildings.
_____
4 We arrived at the hotel at night.
_____
5 I went there because I like the food.
_____
6 They stayed in a youth hostel.

Present continuous

Affirmative

I	am	cooking.
He/She/It	is	eating.
We/You/They	are	reading.

Negative

I	'm not	cooking.
He/She/It	isn't	eating.
We/You/They	aren't	reading.

Use *be* (auxiliary verb) + the *-ing* form of the verb to make the present continuous.

We are / We're cooking.

Contractions

I am cooking.	→	I'm cooking
He is reading.	→	He's reading.
They are sleeping.	→	They're sleeping.

Use the present continuous for activities in progress at the time of speaking.

We're cooking.

She's reading. She isn't watching TV.

He gets up at seven o'clock.

It's seven o'clock. He's getting up.

Questions

Am	I	
Is	he/she/it	reading?
Are	we/you/they	

Short answers

	I	am.
Yes,	he/she/it	is.
	we/you/they	are.
	I	'm not.
No,	he/she/it	isn't.
	we/you/they	aren't.

What	are we/you/they	doing?
Where	is he/she/it	going?

Word order in present continuous questions = (*Wh-* +) *be* + subject + *-ing*

Affirmative =			They're playing.
Question =		Are	they playing?
Wh- question =	What	are	they playing?

What are you doing?

I'm having a cup of coffee.

▶ **Exercises 1, 2, 3 and 4**

Present continuous for the future

I'm meeting my friends	tomorrow.
	on Sunday morning.
	this/next weekend.
	on 8 June.

Use the present continuous + future time expressions for future plans.

We're flying to Rome on 15 June.

▶ **Exercise 5**

Prepositions of place (2)

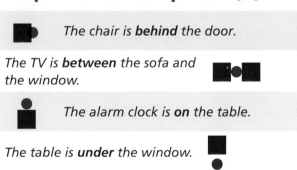

The chair is **behind** the door.

The TV is **between** the sofa and the window.

The alarm clock is **on** the table.

The table is **under** the window.

▶ **Exercise 6**

Exercises

1 Look at the picture of the classroom. Complete the sentences with the correct form of the verbs in brackets.

  1 The teacher *is talking* (talk) to Leon.
  2 Leon _____ (listen) to the teacher.
  3 Two students _____ (write).
  4 Paula _____ (read).
  5 Some students _____ (watch) a video.
  6 Olga _____ (look) out of the window.

2 Write the sentences in Exercise 1 in the negative form.

  1 *The teacher isn't talking to Leon.*
  2
  3
  4
  5
  6

3 Write questions with these words. Write short answers.

  1 you / listen / to me ✓
      Are you listening to me?
      Yes, I am.
  2 Jenni / make coffee ✓

  3 the film / start ✗

  4 the children / play football ✓

  5 you / watch this TV show ✗

  6 David / wash his car ✗

4 Rewrite the sentences in the form given in brackets.

  1 They're making lunch. (question)

  2 He's reading the newspaper. (negative)

  3 Are you watching a video? (affirmative)

  4 We aren't washing the car. (affirmative)

  5 You aren't eating. (question)

  6 Is she sitting on the floor? (negative)

5 Read the sentences. Do they refer to now (N) or the future (F)?

  1 I'm playing tennis on Sunday.
  2 We aren't listening to the radio.
  3 My friends are coming this weekend.
  4 Is your family having dinner together tonight?
  5 What are you doing in June?
  6 My sister is staying with us.

6 Read the sentences about things in a living room. Choose the correct option.

  1 The sofa is *between / under* the door and the window.
  2 There's a cupboard *between / behind* the sofa.
  3 There's a TV *on / under* a small table.
  4 The clock is *between / on* two windows.
  5 There are some flowers *behind / on* the desk.
  6 There's a rug *on / under* the table.

Unit 1

▶ 1

Hello! I'm David.

▶ 2

1 **D:** Hello. I'm David.
   M: Hi. I'm Mireya.
   D: Mireya Mayor?
   M: Yes.

2 **D:** Hi! I'm David Doublet.
   M: Hello.
   D: Oh! You're Mireya!
   M: Yes. I'm Mireya Mayor.

3 **D:** Hello. I'm David Doublet.
   M: I'm Mireya.
   D: Mireya?
   M: Yes. M–I–R–E–Y–A.
   D: Hi. Nice to meet you.

▶ 6

1 **P:** I'm Paula.
   Q: Can you spell Paula?
   P: Yes. P–A–U–L–A.

2 **B:** I'm Bryan.
   Q: Can you spell Bryan?
   B: Yes. B–R–Y–A–N.

3 **S:** I'm Simon.
   Q: Can you spell Simon?
   S: Yes. S–I–M–O–N.

4 **A:** I'm Anna.
   Q: Can you spell Anna?
   A: Yes. A–double N–A.

▶ 9

1	Brazil	Brazilian
2	Egypt	Egyptian
3	Italy	Italian
4	Mexico	Mexican
5	Russia	Russian
6	South Africa	South African
7	Spain	Spanish
8	the United Kingdom	British
9	the United States	American
10	Vietnam	Vietnamese

▶ 14

1 Baseball is American.
2 Pasta is from Italy.
3 Jaguar is British.
4 Flamenco is from Spain.

▶ 15

I = interviewer

I: Anne-Marie, what's your phone number?
A: It's 718 760 7101.
I: 7–1–8, 7–6–0, 7–1–0–1. OK?
A: Yes.
I: Thanks.

▶ 16

I = interviewer

I: Nelson, what's your phone number?
N: My work number is 212 736 3100.

I: 2–1–2, 7–3–6, 3–double 1–0?
N: No, it's 3 –1–double 0.
I: OK. Thanks. What's your home number?
N: My home number is 212 340 2583.
I: 2–1–2, 3–4–0, 2–5–8–3. Thanks.

▶ 17

Hi.
Hello.
Good morning.
Good afternoon.
Good evening.
Goodnight.
Goodbye.
Bye.
See you later.

▶ 18

1 **A:** Good morning, Ramon. How are you?
   R: Fine, thanks. And you?
   A: I'm OK.

2 **R:** Bye, Anne-Marie.
   A: Goodnight, Ramon.

▶ 21

1 **T:** What's this in English?
   S: It's a bag.
   T: Can you spell it?
   S: Yes. B–A–G – bag.
   T: Thanks.

2 **T:** What's this in English?
   S: It's a classroom.
   T: Can you spell classroom?
   S: Yes. C–L–A–double S–R–double–O- M – classroom.
   T: Thanks.

3 **T:** What's this in English?
   S: It's a computer.
   T: Can you spell it?
   S: Yes. C–O–M–P–U–T–E–R – computer.
   T: Thanks.

4 **T:** What's this in English?
   S: It's a notebook.
   T: Can you spell notebook?
   S: Yes. N–O–T–E–B–double O–K – notebook.
   T: Thanks.

5 **T:** What's this in English?
   S: It's a pen.
   T: Can you spell it?
   S: Yes. P–E–N – pen.
   T: Thanks.

6 **T:** What's this in English?
   S: It's a pencil.
   T: Can you spell it?
   S: Yes. P–E–N–C–I–L – pencil.
   T: Thanks.

7 **T:** What's this in English?
   S: It's a phone.
   T: Can you spell phone?

   S: Yes. P–H–O–N–E – phone.
   T: Thanks.

8 **T:** What's this in English?
   S: It's a table.
   T: Can you spell it?
   S: Yes. T–A–B–L–E – table.
   T: Thanks.

▶ 23

1 **T:** Good afternoon, everyone. Sit down, please.

2 **T:** OK. Open your books. Look at page six.

3 **S1:** Hello. Sorry I'm late.
   T: That's OK. Sit down, please.

4 **S2:** Can you repeat that, please?
   T: Yes. Look at page six.

5 **T:** Work in pairs.
   S3: I don't understand.
   T: Work in pairs – two students.

6 **T:** This is a computer.
   S4: Can you spell it, please?

7 **S2:** What's this in English?
   T: It's a phone.
   S2: Thanks.

8 **T:** Do Exercise seven at home. See you next time.
   S1 + 3: Bye.

Unit 2

▶ 26

This is in Vietnam. It's a river. It's morning.

▶ 28

1 Monday
2 Tuesday
3 Wednesday
4 Thursday
5 Friday
6 Saturday
7 Sunday

▶ 30

1 This is Jane. This is Paul. They're Australian.
2 I'm Meera. This is Suri. We're from India.
3 In this photo, I'm with my friend Jack. We're in Egypt.
4 Laura is with Brad, Andy and Jessica. They're on holiday.
5 Monique and Claude are from France. They're French.
6 I'm happy. My friend is happy. We're happy!

▶ 31

1 They're Australian.
2 We're from India.
3 We're in Egypt.
4 They're on holiday.
5 They're French.
6 We're happy!

▶ 32

1 We aren't in Tunisia.
2 It isn't a beach.
3 Brad isn't on a camel.
4 I'm not in this photo.

▶ 34

zero
ten
twenty
thirty
forty
fifty
sixty
seventy
eighty
ninety
one hundred

▶ 35

1 four
2 twenty-three, twenty-nine, sixteen, eleven
3 thirty-seven
4 thirty-one
5 sixteen, forty-five

▶ 36

a It isn't cold! It's thirteen degrees.
b Phew! It's cold this morning! It's two degrees.
c It's thirty-one degrees in London today. That's hot!
d Your temperature is thirty-seven degrees.
e Wow! It's forty-six degrees in Casablanca today. And it's twelve degrees in Copenhagen.

▶ 37

1 It's six degrees in Oslo today. It's cold.
2 It's thirty-five degrees in Sydney today. It's hot.
3 It's nineteen degrees in Lisbon today. It's warm.

▶ 38

G = Greg, L = Lorna

G: Hi! Where are you now? Are you in France?
L: Yes, I am. I'm in the Alps. It's beautiful!
G: Are you OK?
L: No, I'm not. It's two degrees!
G: Wow! Is it cold in your hotel?
L: No, it isn't. The hotel is nice.
G: It's thirty-six degrees in Sydney today.
L: Oh! That's hot!
G: Are Kara and Ona in France?
L: No, they aren't. They're on a beach in Morocco!
G: OK! See you on Friday.

▶ 39

1 Q: Are you OK?
   A: Yes, I am.
2 Q: Is Kara in France?
   A: No, she isn't.
3 Q: Are you and Paul in Sydney?
   A: Yes, we are.
4 Q: Is Greg in London?
   A: No, he isn't.
5 Q: Are Kara and Ona in Morocco?
   A: Yes, they are.
6 Q: Is your hotel nice?
   A: Yes, it is.

▶ 41

1 In London, buses are red.
2 In Hawaii, beaches are black.
3 Cuba is an island. In Cuba, cars are old.
4 In Iceland, the lakes are hot.
5 Lake Geneva is in two countries – Switzerland and France.
6 The Blue Mountains are in Australia.
7 Hong Kong, Shanghai and Beijing are cities in China.
8 Heathrow is an airport in London.

▶ 44

1 My car registration number is PT61 APR.
2 My email address is jamesp@edu.au.
3 My address is 3 Park Street, Gateshead NE2 4AG.
4 Here are your keys.

▶ 45

A = assistant, L = Ms Lopez

A: Good evening.
L: Good evening. My name's Lopez. My car booking is for three days – Tuesday to Thursday.
A: Ah yes, Ms Lopez. What's your first name, please?
L: It's Marta. Here's my ID card – Marta is my first name. Lopez is my surname.
A: Thank you. Where are you from in Mexico, Ms Lopez?
L: I'm from Mexico City.
A: Ah! Is this your address?
L: Yes, it is.
A: OK. Are you on holiday here?
L: No, I'm not. I'm on business.
A: What's your email address, please?
L: It's m lopez at hotmail dot com.
A: OK. Here are your keys. The car is in the car park, number six.
L: Thanks. What's the car registration number?
A: It's on your key – BD61 ATC.
L: Thanks.

Unit 3

▶ 52

A: Is this a photo of your family?
B: Yes, it is.
A: Who's this?
B: She's my sister. Her name's Heelan. It's her wedding.
A: OK. So is this her husband?
B: Yes. His name's Husham.
A: Is this your daughter?
B: Yes. Her name's Nadia.
A: How old is she?
B: She's twelve years old.

▶ 53

Three important people in my life are Elisa, Nuno and Prem.
Elisa's my best friend. She's twenty-three. Elisa's eyes are brown and her hair is black. She's tall. She's nice.
Nuno is my brother. He's my friend too. He's twenty-five years old. My eyes are blue, but Nuno's eyes are green. His hair is brown. He isn't tall. We're both short.
Prem is a friend in my English class. Prem's eyes are brown and his hair is brown too. He's young – he's seventeen!

▶ 54

1 Ana is Nuno's sister.
2 Elisa is Ana's friend.
3 Prem is Ana's classmate.
4 Ana's eyes are blue.
5 Prem's school is The English Academy.
6 Ana's friends are Elisa, Nuno and Prem.

▶ 55

1 January
2 February
3 March
4 April
5 May
6 June
7 July
8 August
9 September
10 October
11 November
12 December

▶ 58

1 My children are boys.
2 Andy and David are the men in my family.
3 The people in my class are Spanish and Italian.
4 Rosa, Lidia and Ana are women in my class.

▶ 60

A: Congratulations!

B: Thank you. We're very happy.

A: Ah, she's lovely. What's her name?

B: It's Juba.

A: Hello, Juba.

▶ 61

1 **D = Diana E = Edward**

E: Hello!

D: Hello, Edward. Come in.

E: Happy New Year!

D: Happy New Year to you too! Come and say hello to my family.

2 **F = Freya, G = Gloria**

G: Happy Birthday, Freya.

F: Thank you.

G: How old are you? Nineteen or twenty?

F: Actually, I'm twenty-one.

G: Oh great! When's the party?

F: It's on Saturday.

3 **A = Adam, E = Emma, J = James**

A: Congratulations, Emma and James!

E + J: Thank you very much.

A: I'm very happy for you. Here's a card and a present for you.

E: Thank you!

A: Your dress is beautiful, Emma!

E: Thanks.

▶ 63

C = Celia, E = Elena

C: Hello, Elena. It's nice to see you. Come in.

E: Hi, Celia. This is for the baby.

C: Oh, that's very kind. Thank you very much.

E: You're welcome. Now, where *is* the baby?

C: She's with my mother.

Unit 4

▶ 66

Kazakhstan is in Asia. The new capital city of Kazakhstan is called Astana. The word 'Astana' means 'capital' in the Kazakh language. The buildings in Astana are tall and new. At night, they are different colours – red, blue, purple, yellow and green. Astana is a clean and modern city. Tourists visit the parks in Astana.

▶ 67

1 a park

2 a car park

3 a café

4 a market

5 an information centre

6 a bus station

7 a train station

8 a bank

9 a museum

10 a cinema

▶ 68

1 A: Excuse me?

B: Yes?

A: Where's the train station?

B: It's in Exeter Street.

A: Is it near here?

B: Yes, it is.

A: OK. Thanks.

2 C: Excuse me?

D: Yes?

C: Is the information centre near here?

D: Yes, it is. It's near the park.

C: OK. Thanks.

3 E: Excuse me?

F: Yes?

E: Is the car park in this street?

F: No, it isn't. This is Exeter Street. The car park's in Oxford Street. It's next to the park.

E: Thank you very much.

4 G: Excuse me?

H: Yes?

G: Where's the bank?

H: I'm not sure. Oh! It's opposite the museum.

G: Is it near here?

H: Yes, it is.

G: OK. Thanks.

▶ 69

T = tourist, A = Tourist Information Centre assistant

1 T1: Hi.

A: Good morning.

T1: Is this a map of the city?

A: No, it isn't. That's a map of England. This is a map of London.

T1: OK… And where's the London Eye?

A: It's near the River Thames … here it is.

T1: Oh, yes. Is it open on Sunday?

A: Yes, it's open every day.

2 T2: Good afternoon. Where are the timetables, please?

A: Well, these are train timetables, here.

T2: And bus timetables?

A: Those are bus timetables, next to the door.

T2: OK, thanks.

▶ 70

1 A: Is this a train timetable?

B: No, it's a bus timetable.

2 A: Excuse me. Are these pens or pencils?

B: I'm not sure … Oh, yes. They're pencils. The pens are next to the maps.

A: OK, thanks.

3 A: Excuse me. Are those maps of London?

B: Yes, they are.

4 A: Is that guidebook in English?

B: Which guidebook?

A: The book next to you.

B: No, it isn't. It's in Spanish.

▶ 73

a It's eleven o'clock.

b It's nine thirty.

c It's four fifteen.

d It's seven forty-five.

e It's eight twenty.

f It's three fifty-five.

▶ 74

1 What time is it?

It's five o'clock.

2 What time is it?

It's one thirty.

3 What time is it?

It's seven fifteen.

4 What time is it?

It's nine forty-five.

5 What time is it?

It's two twenty.

6 What time is it?

It's six o'clock.

▶ 75

1 A: Where are your children? Are they here?

B: No. It's two o'clock – they're at school.

2 C: Sandy, what time is your train?

S: It's at five o'clock.

3 D: Hi Tom. Are you at work?

T: No, I'm not. It's a holiday today. I'm at home.

▶ 77

a mineral water

b fruit juice

c cake

d coffee

e salad

f tea

g sandwich

h apple

i banana

j orange

▶ 78

1 A: Hi. Can I help you?

C: Two coffees, please.

A: Large or small?

C: Small.

A: Anything else?

C: No, thanks.

2 A: Hi. Can I help you?

C: Can I have a mineral water, please?

A: Anything else?

C: Yes. A salad.

A: OK. Four euros, please.

3 **A:** Can I help you?

C: A tea and a fruit juice, please.

A: Anything else?

C: Yes. Two cakes, please.

A: OK. Here you are. Seven pounds please.

Unit 5

▶ 82

Look at this fantastic photo. This is a man in the air. His name's Yves Rossy. He's also called *Jetman* – he can fly. Rossy is from Switzerland. In the photo, Rossy is in the air near mountains in Switzerland. He's in the air for five minutes. It's great!

▶ 84

1 Robots can move.

2 Robots can speak.

3 Robots can carry things.

4 People can't fly.

5 I can speak English.

6 My grandfather can't run.

▶ 86

C = Christine, L = Lewis

L: Hi. Welcome to 'Technology Today'. I'm Lewis Jones and today I'm with Christine Black, a robot expert, and Tomo, a Japanese robot. Hi, Christine.

C: Hi, Lewis.

L: Christine, tell me about this robot.

C: Well, Tomo is from Japan. She's a new kind of robot. She can do things that people can do.

L: 'She'? Or 'it'?

C: Aha! We say 'she'. *She's* a robot.

L: OK. So, *she's* from Japan. Can she speak Japanese?

C: Oh yes, she can speak Japanese and English.

L: OK. Can she sing?

C: Yes, she can.

L: And can she play the piano?

C: Yes, she can.

L: Wow! I can't sing or play the piano. Can she swim?

C: Well, Tomo can't swim, but some robots can swim.

L: OK. Well, my last question is about the name. What does 'Tomo' mean?

C: It means 'intelligent' in Japanese.

L: OK, Christine, thanks very much.

C: Thanks!

▶ 87

a a cat

b a football

c photos

d a motorbike

e a watch

f a guitar

g a camera

h glasses

▶ 88

1 I can play the guitar. I have three guitars. This one is interesting. It has a date on it – 1921. It's very old.

2 This is our cat. He's called Dylan. He's nine years old. He has different coloured eyes. One is green and one is blue. He's beautiful.

3 I can't see without my glasses! These are my new glasses. The astronauts at NASA have the same glasses. They're very expensive.

4 I have a very interesting football. It's from the 2014 Football World Cup. It's from a game between Portugal and Germany. It has Cristiano Ronaldo's signature on it.

▶ 89

1 I have a bike.

2 My friend has a motorbike.

3 My brother has two cameras.

4 My sister has a bag.

5 My friends have a car.

6 I have two sisters. They have brown eyes.

▶ 91

a two pounds thirty

b thirteen pounds fifty

c fifteen euros

d three euros seventy-five

e seventeen dollars eighty cents

f eighteen dollars

▶ 92

1 It's thirty pounds.

2 It's forty pounds.

3 It's fifteen pounds.

4 It's sixteen pounds.

5 It's seventy pounds.

6 It's eighteen pounds.

▶ 93

1 **A:** Can I help you?

C: How much is this alarm clock?

A: That's a clock radio. It's fifty euros.

C: Hmm, that's a bit expensive. Thanks.

A: That's OK. No problem.

2 **A:** Can I help you?

C: Yes, I'd like these sunglasses, please.

A: Certainly.

C: Oh! Are they for men or women?

A: They're for men.

C: That's great.

A: OK, that's ninety-five pounds fifty, please.

C: Here you are.

3 **C:** Excuse me.

A: Yes, can I help you?

C: How much are these memory sticks?

A: They're five ninety-nine each.

C: Can I pay with euros?

A: Yes, of course.

Unit 6

▶ 96

These people love their sport. They aren't players – they're fans. Their team is called the Kaizer Chiefs. Football and rugby are popular sports in South Africa. Football is an international sport – about 270 million people play football in about 200 countries. The football World Cup is every four years. The World Cup prize is millions of dollars – $30 million at the World Cup in South Africa.

▶ 97

1 Running is a sport in the Olympic Games.

2 Swimming is a sport in water.

3 Cycling is a sport with bikes.

4 Tennis is a sport with a ball for two or four people.

5 Basketball is a sport with a ball for two teams.

▶ 99

1 I like tennis.

2 I like swimming.

3 I don't like football.

4 My friends like sport.

5 I don't like basketball.

6 We like Formula 1.

▶ 100

Q: Hi. Can I ask you some questions about sport?

A: Yes, of course.

Q: Thanks. Do you like sport?

A: Yes, I do. I love sport!

Q: What sports do you like?

A: My favourite sports are tennis and football.

Q: Tennis and football … thank you.

▶ 101

1 **Q:** Hello. Can I ask you some questions?

B: OK. What about?

Q: About sport. Do people in your family like sport?

B: No, we don't. Well, we like sport on TV.

Q: OK. What sports do you like on TV?

B: Oh, football and Formula 1.

Q: Thank you.

2 **Q:** Hi. Can I ask you some questions about sport?

C: OK.

Q: Thanks. Do you like basketball?

C: No, I don't.

Q: Do you like swimming or cycling?

C: No, I don't. I don't like sport!

Q: Oh!

▶ 102

1 Do you like sport?

2 What sports do you like?

▶ 103

Comedies are films.

Detective stories are books.

Fish are animals.

Pop is a type of music.

Scuba diving is a sport.

Wildlife shows are TV shows.

▶ 105

1 He likes fish.

2 He likes Botswana.

3 He doesn't like cold places.

4 He likes water.

5 He likes coffee.

▶ 106

a fruit

b cheese

c eggs

d meat

e bread

f pasta

g vegetables

h potatoes

▶ 108

1 **A:** Let's play table tennis tomorrow.

B: No, thanks. I don't like table tennis.

A: OK. Let's watch football on TV.

B: I'm sorry. I don't like sport very much. It's boring.

2 **C:** Let's go to the cinema this weekend.

D: That's a good idea. What's on?

C: A film with Felicity Jones. It's on at seven o'clock and nine o'clock.

D: Oh, I love her. She's fantastic.

3 **E:** Let's have fish tonight.

F: I'm sorry. I don't like fish. It's horrible.

E: OK. How about pizza? Do you like pizza?

F: Yes, it's great. Let's invite my sister and her husband.

E: OK. Send them a text message.

▶ 109

Sport's boring.

She's fantastic.

It's horrible.

Pizza's great.

Unit 7

▶ 112

The Holi festival – or festival of colours – is in March. It's a very happy festival. It's a celebration of spring and new life. People say 'goodbye' to winter and 'hello' to spring. In India, the winter months are December, January and February. The Holi festival is one or two days. It's a big celebration in parts of India and in other parts of the world.

▶ 114

1 I get up at six o'clock.

2 I have breakfast at six thirty.

3 I start work at seven o'clock.

4 I have lunch in a café.

5 I finish work at five forty-five.

6 I have dinner at home.

7 I go to bed at eleven thirty.

▶ 116

I'm Roberto. I'm married and I have two children. I work in an observatory in Chile. I start work at nine o'clock at night. I finish work at 2.30 in the morning and I go home and go to bed. At eight o'clock, I get up and I have breakfast with my wife and children. They go to school at 8.30. They don't go to school on Saturday and Sunday.

▶ 117

1 reading

2 cooking

3 dancing

4 singing

5 painting

6 walking

7 climbing

8 shopping

▶ 118

I = interviewer

1 **I:** Andy, do you have any hobbies?

A: Yes, I do – dressing up! My friends and I dress up as Vikings.

I: Do you dress up every week?

A: No, we don't. We dress up in January. We go to a big festival in Shetland. It's called Up Helly Aa. It's exciting.

2 **I:** Tina, what are your hobbies?

T: My hobby is singing. In my free time, I sing in a band with two friends. It's fun. In summer, we go to different towns. I like it.

I: Do your friends sing?

T: No, they don't. They play the guitar and the piano.

3 **I:** Naga, do you have any hobbies?

N: I don't have many hobbies. I like cooking. I enjoy making cakes for my family. I cook in the evening. It's nice.

I: Do you eat your cakes?

N: Yes, I do. Chocolate cake is my favourite.

4 **I:** Paul, what are your hobbies?

P: My hobbies are painting and listening to music. I paint with a group of friends. We meet on Saturdays. We're in a club. It's interesting.

I: Do you paint pictures of people?

P: Yes, we do.

▶ 119

1 **I:** Do you dress up every week?

A: No, we don't. We dress up in January.

2 **I:** Do your friends sing?

T: No, they don't. They play the guitar and the piano.

3 **I:** Do you eat your cakes?

N: Yes, I do. Chocolate cake is my favourite.

4 **I:** Do you paint pictures of people?

P: Yes, we do.

▶ 120

1 Do you enjoy shopping?

2 Do you read newspapers?

3 Do your friends go dancing?

4 Do you and your friends play basketball?

5 Do you go climbing?

6 Do you and your friends watch TV?

▶ 122

1 I live in Canada. My favourite time of year is winter. It's cold and snowy.

2 I live in South Africa. I like spring. It's sunny and it isn't cold.

3 I live in the north of Australia. Summer is the wet season. It's hot and rainy. I don't like it!

4 I live in the United Kingdom. It's autumn here. It's cloudy. It's windy too, but I like it. We don't have a dry season.

▶ 124

1 Ooh, I'm cold.

2 I'm tired.

3 I'm thirsty.

4 Ugh, I'm hot.

5 Ugh, I'm wet.

6 I'm bored.

7 Mmm, I'm hungry.

▶ 125

M = mother, F = father, P = Paul,
A = Anna

M: What's the matter?
F: It's cold and I'm thirsty.
M: Why don't you have a cup of tea? Here you are.
F: Thanks. Paul, are you OK?
P: No, I'm not. I don't feel well.
M: Why don't you eat a sandwich? Here.
P: No, thanks. I'm not hungry. I'm cold and I'm wet.
A: [groans]
M: What's the matter, Anna?
A: I'm bored.
M: Why don't you go to the beach? Go swimming.
A: In the rain?!? Mum!
M: I don't understand you all. We're on holiday!

▶ 126

Why don't you have a cup of tea?
I don't feel well.
I don't understand you all.

Unit 8

▶ 129

I = interviewer, M = man

I: Do you like your job?
M: Yes, I love my job. I don't work in an office. I work outside. Every day is different in my job.
I: What do you do?
M: I'm a painter. It's an interesting job. I work with a big company. I don't paint houses. I paint ships.

▶ 131

Lily goes to different Tube stations. She doesn't drive a train. She's a police officer. Lily walks around stations. She helps people with problems. Sometimes, she works in a big office. Lily watches the trains on computer screens and she looks at the cameras.

▶ 132

Naveen enjoys his job.
Lily goes to stations.
Lily helps people.
Lily works in a big office.

▶ 134

Q: Why is the school for girls and not boys?
A: In Kenya, in villages, girls don't usually go to school.
Q: And do the girls live at the school?
A: Yes, they do, because it's a long way to their homes and villages.
Q: Does the school have many students?

A: Yes, about two hundred.
Q: Does Kakenya work at the school?
A: Yes, she does.
Q: What does she do?
A: She's the president of the school.
Q: Does she teach?
A: Yes, she does. She sometimes teaches primary school subjects.
Q: And tell me about the students.

▶ 136

1 R: Good morning. PJ International. Can I help you?
   C: Yes, can I speak to Ed Smith, please?
   R: I'm sorry. He's in a meeting.
   C: OK. Thank you. I'll call back later. Goodbye.
   R: Goodbye.
2 R: Hello. Green Wildlife Park. Can I help you?
   C: Good morning. Can I speak to Mr Watts, please?
   R: Yes, one moment, please.
   C: Thank you.
3 R: Good morning. City College. Can I help you?
   C: Yes, can I speak to Mrs Jackson, please?
   R: I'm sorry. She's out of the office at the moment.
   C: OK. Thank you. I'll call back later. Goodbye.
   R: Goodbye.

▶ 137

1 R: Good morning. PJ International. Can I help you?
   C: Yes, can I speak to Ed Smith, please?
   R: I'm sorry. He's in a meeting.
   C: OK. Thank you. I'll call back later. Goodbye.
   R: Goodbye.
3 R: Good morning. City College. Can I help you?
   C: Yes, can I speak to Mrs Jackson, please?
   R: I'm sorry. She's out of the office at the moment.
   C: OK. Thank you. I'll call back later. Goodbye.
   R: Goodbye.

Unit 9

▶ 141

1 I travel from Paris to London for my job. I go every week. I usually go by train because I can work on the train.
2 I'm an Australian student and I travel in my holidays. I love Asia! I travel by bus. It's really interesting. You meet a lot of people.

3 I live in San Francisco. I don't like flying, so I never travel by plane. I don't really travel.
4 I'm from Madrid, but my parents live in Mallorca. I visit them every summer. I usually go by boat.

▶ 144

My suitcase is very small, but that's OK. I only take things I need. My next trip is to Hong Kong. I'm ready to go. So, what's in my suitcase? Well, there's my laptop, of course. And there are two shirts for work and also there's a skirt. There's a dress for the evening and there's a pair of shoes. I like shoes for the day and different shoes for the evening. And finally, there are some T-shirts. That's all I need.

▶ 145

There are two shirts.
There are some books.
There are three scarves.
There are some T-shirts.

▶ 146

1 TV
2 bath
3 bed
4 chair
5 table
6 lamp
7 desk
8 sofa
9 wardrobe
10 armchair
11 shower
12 fridge

▶ 147

S = Sandra, L = Luca

S: OK, that's the flight. Now let's look for a hotel. Is it for two nights or three?
L: Three nights – Friday, Saturday and Sunday. Are there any hotels near the airport?
S: Yes, there are. There are two or three, I think. Oh! This one's expensive!
L: Is there a cheap hotel near the airport?
S: No, there aren't any cheap hotels near the airport.
L: OK. Let's look in the city centre. Are there any cheap hotels there?
S: Yes, of course there are.
L: Well, that's good. And is there a bus to the city centre?
S: A bus from the airport? Yes, there is. There's a bus every twenty minutes from the airport to the centre. There isn't a train, but that's OK.
L: And there are taxis too.
S: I think the bus is fine. OK, so let's look at these hotels.

▶ 149

R: Good afternoon. Can I help you?

G1: Hello. We'd like a room for two nights.

R: Of course. Can I have your name, please? And a credit card?

G1: Here you are. My name's on the card.

R: OK. That's fine. Your room is 137.

G1: Thanks. I'd like help with these bags.

R: That's no problem. Just a moment.

G2: And is there a restaurant?

R: Yes, there is. It's open from 7 to 10 for breakfast and 6 to 11 in the evening.

G1: Can you tell me the wi-fi password?

R: Certainly. It's the name of the hotel – sunhotel. That's one word.

G1: Thanks. And can you call a taxi, please?

R: Yes, of course. Do you want it now?

G1: No, we'd like it for two o'clock.

R: OK.

▶ 150

We'd like a room for two nights.
I'd like help with these bags.
We'd like it for two o'clock.

Unit 10

▶ 153

This is a photo of Ayrton Senna, the famous Formula One driver. Senna was Brazilian. He was the Formula One world champion three times, in 1988, 1990 and 1991. This photo is from 1994. Senna is in Italy. The photo is from just before his last Formula One race.

▶ 155

Nelson Mandela lived from 1918 to 2013.
John Lennon lived from 1940 to 1980.
Isabel Allende was born in 1942.
Angela Merkel was born in 1954.
Ayrton Senna lived from 1960 to 1994.
Malala Yousafzai was born in 1997.

▶ 156

The first round-the-world expedition was from 1519 to 1522. The expedition captain was Ferdinand Magellan .

The first successful South Pole expedition was in 1911. The expedition leader was Roald Amundsen .

The first man in space was Yuri Gagarin. The first woman in space was Valentina Tereshkova. They were both from Russia.

The first woman at the top of Everest was Junko Tabei on 16 May 1975.

The first woman at the North Pole was Ann Bancroft on 1 May 1986.

▶ 157

1 Yuri Gagarin was born in 1934.

2 His parents were farmers.

3 He was a pilot.

▶ 158

first	eleventh
second	twelfth
third	thirteenth
fourth	fourteenth
fifth	fifteenth
sixth	sixteenth
seventh	seventeenth
eighth	eighteenth
ninth	nineteenth
tenth	twentieth

▶ 159

the first of May 1986
the second of June 1953
the third of November 1957
the fourth of October 1957
the twelfth of April 1961
the thirteenth of December 1972
the fourteenth of December 1911
the sixteenth of May, 1975
the twentieth of July 1969

▶ 161

1 **I = interviewer, J = Joe**

I: Joe, who was important to you when you were young?

J: Well, I love animals. I remember David Attenborough and his programmes about animals.

I: Was he on TV?

J: Yes, he was.

I: Were the programmes only for children?

J: No, they weren't. They were for everyone.

I: Can you remember your favourite David Attenborough programme?

J: I think it was a programme about meerkats. They were really funny! I love animals and science.

2 **I = interviewer, A = Aneta**

I: Aneta, who was important to you when you were young?

A: Well, I love reading. English was my favourite subject at school. My favourite book was *Frankenstein*.

I: Who was the writer of *Frankenstein*?

A: It was Mary Shelley. She was a very clever woman and a great writer.

I: And were you good at English?

A: Yes, I was.

▶ 162

I = interviewer, A = Olga

I: Olga, who was important to you when you were young?

O: I remember Michael Johnson. He was a great sportsman.

I: Was he an Olympic champion?

O: Yes, he was. Four times. The last time was in 2000.

I: Were the 2000 Olympics in Beijing?

O: No, they weren't. They were in Sydney.

I: Were you good at sports at school?

O: Yes, I was. I was in the basketball team at school.

▶ 164

1 **T = teacher, S = student**

T: Hello!

S: Hi, I'm sorry I'm late. The train was late.

T: That's OK. Take a seat.

2 C: Oh hi, Ravi.

R: Hi, Clare.

C: Erm, the meeting was at 2.30. Where were you?

R: Oh, I'm sorry. I was very busy.

C: It's OK. It wasn't an important meeting.

3 A: Mmm, this coffee is good!

B: Yes, it is.

A: So, what about yesterday? We were at your house at ten o'clock. Where were you?

B: I'm very sorry. We weren't at home. We were at my sister's house!

A: It's OK. Don't worry.

▶ 165

1 I'm sorry I'm late.

2 The train was late.

3 I was very busy.

4 We weren't at home.

Unit 11

▶ 168

The city of Timbuktu in Mali is famous for its books and documents. Timbuktu was a centre of learning for hundreds of years. There were thousands of documents on mathematics, science, art and other subjects. Lots of the books and documents were in libraries and in family homes. Some books are four hundred years old.

▶ **170**

The scientists at the University of Innsbruck started their investigation. It was a man. They called him 'Ötzi' because the body was in the Ötztal mountains in the Alps. The scientists finished their report about Ötzi. He lived about 5,000 years ago. He was a small man. He was about forty-five years old when he died. The scientists think an arrow killed Ötzi.

▶ **172**

1 My friend walked across the Alps in 2016.
2 I started my English course last year.
3 My mother lived in Italy from 2009 to 2015.
4 Our holiday finished last Sunday.

▶ **173**

I = Interviewer, D = Dinah

I: Hi, Dinah. New Orleans is very important in your life. Were you born there?
D: Yes, I was.
I: And did you live there when you were a child?
D: Yes, I did. I went to school there and I went to university there too. My father and his grandparents were born in New Orleans too. So the city is very important in my family's history.
I: What did you want to be when you were a child?
D: I wanted to be an artist. My parents are both artists.
I: Did you study art at university?
D: No, actually, I didn't study art! I studied music.
I: Why did you decide to be a musician?
D: Music is part of the story of my city. And now I write songs about the people from my city. They tell me their stories – all about their lives in New Orleans – and I sing about them.

▶ **174**

1 Did you study English at school?
2 Did you meet your best friend at school?
3 Did you live in a big city when you were young?
4 Did you leave school when you were eighteen?
5 Did you start work last year?
6 Did you go on holiday every year?

▶ **176**

1 A: Did you and Sonia have a good time in Sydney last week?
  B: Yes, thanks, we did. But we didn't go swimming.
  A: Oh? Why not?
  B: There was a shark in the sea!

2 C: Did you and Jack have a good holiday last year?
  D: No, we didn't.
  C: Oh? Why not?
  D: Well, we stayed at home. We didn't have any money!

3 E: Did you and Anita have a nice meal last night?
  F: Yes, we did. It was delicious. And we didn't pay!
  E: Oh? Why not?
  F: My boss paid!

▶ **177**

1 We didn't go swimming.
2 We didn't have any money.
3 We didn't pay!

Unit 12

▶ **180**

A: I love the weekend. I get up late and go shopping in town.
B: Oh, I never get up late at the weekend. I play football on Saturday morning and we start at eight o'clock.
C: I usually get up late on Sunday but not on Saturday. On Sunday, I sometimes meet friends and we go out for a meal.
A: Yes, me too. But I go out for a meal with my family. We always go to the same place. I love family Sunday lunch!

▶ **181**

1	a cooker, a fridge	a kitchen
2	a chair, a table	a dining room
3	an armchair, a sofa	a living room
4	a bed, a wardrobe	a bedroom
5	a bath, a shower, a toilet	a bathroom

▶ **183**

Q: Tell us about these photos of Ayu's family.
A: Well, this is Ayu's mother. She's in the kitchen. She's cooking.
Q: What's she making?
A: She's making lunch. They have a big family lunch every Saturday.
Q: And who's this?
A: That's Ayu's husband, Amir, in the bathroom. He's bathing their daughter.
Q: How old is their daughter?
A: She's eighteen months old. And this is Ayu's father with his friend. They're talking and drinking coffee.
Q: Are they sitting outside or inside?
A: They're inside. And then this photo is Amir's brother with his son.
Q: What are they doing? Are they reading?
A: No, they aren't. They're playing a game on Amir's computer.

Q: And what about this last one?
A: This is Ayu's brother – he's wearing an orange T-shirt – and his friend. They're washing their motorbikes. They do that every Saturday.
Q: Which is your favourite photo?
A: Oh, I think it's the one of Ayu's husband and daughter because they are both smiling and happy.

▶ **184**

A: What are you doing next weekend?
B: I'm not sure. My brother is coming tomorrow.
A: Is he staying the weekend?
B: Yes, he is. We're going out for a meal on Saturday evening.
A: Helen Smith is giving a talk on Sunday afternoon. Do you want to come?
B: Yes, that's a great idea.

▶ **185**

1 What are you doing this weekend?
2 Are they doing their homework?
3 I'm going shopping.
4 We're going out for a meal.

▶ **188**

G = George, S = Samira, K = Kris

G: Samira, would you like a drink? A cup of tea or coffee? Kris? What about you?
S: Yes, please. I'd like a cup of tea.
K: Tea for me too. So, George, when are you moving to your new house?
G: On Monday. We're having our last lunch in our old house on Sunday. Would you like to come?
S: OK, great!
K: Sorry, I can't make it! I'd like to come, but I'm going on holiday on Sunday.
G: Well, do you want to have lunch in our new house? How about next month?
K: OK, great. After next Saturday is fine.

▶ **189**

1 Would you like to come?
2 Would you like to sit down?
3 Would you like a snack?
4 Would you like a drink?

NATIONAL GEOGRAPHIC
L E A R N I N G

Life Beginner Student's Book, 2nd Edition
Helen Stephenson, John Hughes,
Paul Dummett

Vice President, Editorial Director:
John McHugh

Executive Editor: Sian Mavor

Publishing Consultant: Karen Spiller

Project Managers: Sarah Ratcliff, Laura Brant

Development Editor: Liz Driscoll

Editorial Manager: Claire Merchant

Head of Strategic Marketing ELT:
Charlotte Ellis

Senior Content Project Manager:
Nick Ventullo

Manufacturing Buyer: Elaine Bevan

Senior IP Analyst: Michelle McKenna

IP Project Manager: Carissa Poweleit

Cover: Lisa Trager

Text design: emc design ltd.

Compositor: emc design ltd.

Audio: Tom Dick and Debbie Productions Ltd

For product information and technology assistance, contact us at
Cengage Learning Customer & Sales Support, cengage.com/contact

For permission to use material from this text or product,
submit all requests online at **cengage.com/permissions**
Further permissions questions can be emailed to
permissionrequest@cengage.com

ISBN: 978-1-337-28528-5

National Geographic Learning
Cheriton House, North Way,
Andover, Hampshire, SP10 5BE
United Kingdom

National Geographic Learning, a Cengage Learning Company, has a mission to bring the world to the classroom and the classroom to life. With our English language programs, students learn about their world by experiencing it. Through our partnerships with National Geographic and TED Talks, they develop the language and skills they need to be successful global citizens and leaders.

Locate your local office at **international.cengage.com/region**

Visit National Geographic Learning online at **NGL.Cengage.com/ELT**
Visit our corporate website at **www.cengage.com**

CREDITS

Text: pp 9–10: recording: David Doubilet; p10: recording Mireya Mayor; p15: source: 'Map "Ring Around N.Y.C."', National Geographic, 2009, page 6; p72: sources: 'Interview with Zeb Hogan', National Geographic Kids, and 'Freshwater Hero: Zeb Hogan', National Geographic; p96: sources: 'Explorer Bio: Kakenya Ntaiya', National Geographic, and 'Video "Kakenya Ntaiya", Educator and Activist', National Geographic; p99: sources: 'Tigers', by Caroline Alexander, National Geographic, December 2011, and 'Africa Vet's "House Calls" Aid Wild Cats, Film Reveals', by Brian Handwerk, National Geographic Ultimate Explorer, January 23, 2004; p111: source: 'Road-Tripping the Trans-Siberian Highway', by McKenzie Funk, National Geographic Adventure, June/July 2008; p130: sources: 'Last Hours of the Iceman', by Stephen Hall, National Geographic, September 2007, 'Iceman Autopsy', by Stephen Hall, National Geographic, November 2011, 'Who killed the Iceman?', National Geographic, February 2000, and https://en.wikipedia.org/wiki/Ötzi; p132: source: 'Explorer Bio: Caroline Gerdes', National Geographic; p135: source: 'Stone Forest', by Neil Shea, National Geographic, November 2009; p147: source: 'Saving Energy Starts at Home', National Geographic, March 2009.
Cover: © Miao Jian/Wuhan Morning Post/VCG/Getty Images.
Photos: 6 (tl) © Roger Ressmeyer/Corbis/VCG/Getty Images; 6 (tr) Mr Standfast/Alamy Stock Photo; 6 (b) Karol Kozlowski/Alamy Stock Photo; 7 (t) © Eric CHRETIEN/Gamma-Rapho/Getty Images; 7 (bl) © Michael Nichols/National Geographic Creative; 7 (br) © Jill Schneider/National Geographic Creative; 8 (tl) © David Doubilet/National Geographic Creative; 8 (tm) imageBROKER/Alamy Stock Photo; 8 (tr) © Medford Taylor/National Geographic Creative; 8 (mtl) © Gerd Ludwig/National Geographic Creative; 8 (mtm) © Laurent Gillieron/AFP/Getty Images; 8 (mtr) © Lefty Shivambu/Gallo Images/Getty Images; 8 (mbl) © Dibyangshu Sarkar/AFP/Getty Images; 8 (mbm) © Zay Yar Lin; 8 (mbr) © Michael S. Lewis/National Geographic Creative; 8 (bl) © Dario Mitidieri/Getty Images; 8 (bm) © Brent Stirton/Getty Images; 8 (br) © Lynsey Addario/National Geographic Creative; 9 © David Doubilet/National Geographic Creative; 10 (l) © Mauricio Handler/National Geographic Creative; 10 (r) © Mark Thiessen/National Geographic Creative; 11 (tl) © Ryan McVay/Getty Images; 11 (tr) © Future Publishing/Getty Images; 11 (ml) © Ozaiachin/Shutterstock.com; 11 (mr) © Fotosoroka/Shutterstock.com; 11 (bl) © Carlos E. Santa Maria/Shutterstock.com; 11 (br) Julia Bellack/Alamy Stock Photo; 12 (t) Andrey Arkusha/Alamy Stock Photo; 12 (b) Gallo Images/Alamy Stock Photo; 13 (left col: tl) Terry Allen/Alamy Stock Photo; 13 (left col: tr) © Ilya Andriyanov/Shutterstock.com; 13 (left col: bl) Larry Lilac/Alamy Stock Photo; 13 (left col: br) Blend Images/Alamy Stock Photo; 13 (right

Printed in Greece by Bakis SA
Print Number: 01 Print Year: 2017

ACKNOWLEDGEMENTS

The *Life* publishing team would like to thank the following teachers and students who provided invaluable and detailed feedback on the first edition:
Armik Adamians, Colombo Americano, Cali; Carlos Alberto Aguirre, Universidad Madero, Puebla; Anabel Aikin, La Escuela Oficial de Idiomas de Coslada, Madrid, Spain; Pamela Alvarez, Colegio Eccleston, Lanús; Manuel Antonio, CEL – Unicamp, São Paolo; Bob Ashcroft, Shonan Koka University; Linda Azzopardi, Clubclass; Éricka Bauchwitz, Universidad Madero, Puebla, Mexico; Paola Biancolini, Università Cattolica del Sacro Cuore, Milan; Laura Bottiglieri, Universidad Nacional de Salta; Richard Brookes, Brookes Talen, Aalsmeer; Maria Cante, Universidad Madero, Puebla; Carmín Castillo, Universidad Madero, Puebla; Ana Laura Chacón, Universidad Madero, Puebla; Somchao Chatnaridom, Suratthani Rajabhat University, Surat Thani; Adrian Cini, British Study Centres, London; Andrew Clarke, Centre of English Studies, Dublin; Mariano Cordoni, Centro Universitario de Idiomas, Buenos Aries; Monica Cuellar, Universidad La Gran Colombia, Colombia; Jacqui Davis-Bowen, St Giles International; Nuria Mendoza Dominguez, Universidad Nebrija, Madrid; Robin Duncan, ITC London; Christine Eade, Libera Università Internazionale degli Studi Sociali Guido Carli, Rome; Leopoldo Pinzon Escobar, Universidad Catolica; Joanne Evans, Linguarama, Berlin; Juan David Figueroa, Colombo Americano, Cali; Emmanuel Flores, Universidad del Valle de Puebla; Sally Fryer, University of Sheffield, Sheffield; Antonio David Berbel García, Escuela Oficial de Idiomas de Almería, Spain; Lia Gargioni, Feltrinelli Secondary School, Milan; Roberta Giugni, Galileo Galilei Secondary School, Legnano; Monica Gomez, Universidad Pontificia Bolivariana; Doctor Erwin Gonzales, Centro de Idiomas Universidad Nacional San Agustin, Peru; Ivonne Gonzalez, Universidad de La Sabana; J Gouman, Pieter Zandt Scholengemeenschap, Kampen; Cherryll Harrison, UNINT, Rome; Lottie Harrison, International House Recoleta; Marjo Heij, CSG Prins Maurits, Middelharnis; María del Pilar Hernández, Universidad Madero, Puebla; Luz Stella Hernandez, Universidad de La Sabana, Colombia; Rogelio Herrera, Colombo Americano, Cali; Amy Huang, Language Canada, Taipei,; Huang Huei-Jiun, Pu Tai Senior High School; Nelson Jaramillo, Colombo Americano, Cali; Jacek Kaczmarek, Xiehe YouDe High School, Taipei; Thurgadevi Kalay, Kaplan, Singapore; Noreen Kane, Centre of English Studies, Dublin; Billy Kao, Jinwen University of Science and Technology; Shih-Fan Kao, Jinwen University of Science and Technology, Taipei; Youmay Kao, Mackay Junior College of Medicine, Nursing, and Management, Taipei, Taiwan; Fleur Kelder, Vechtstede College, Weesp; Dr Sarinya Khattiya, Chiang Mai University; Lucy Khoo, Kaplan; Karen Koh, Kaplan, Singapore; Susan Langerfeld, Liceo Scientifico Statale Augusto Righi, Rome; Hilary Lawler, Centre of English Studies, Dublin; Eva Lendi, Kantonsschule Zürich Nord, Zürich; Evon Lo, Jinwen University of Science and Technology, Taiwan; Peter Loftus, Centre of English Studies, Dublin; José Luiz, Inglês com Tecnologia, Cruzeiro; Christopher MacGuire, UC Language Center, Chile; Eric Maher, Centre of English Studies, Dublin; Nick Malewski, ITC London; Claudia Maribell Loo, Universidad Madero, Puebla; Malcolm Marr, ITC London; Graciela Martin, ICANA (Belgrano); Erik Meek, CS Vincent van Gogh, Assen,; Marlene Merkt, Kantonsschule Zürich Nord, Zürich; David Moran, Qatar University, Doha; Rosella Morini, Feltrinelli Secondary School, Milan; Judith Mundell, Quarenghi Adult Learning Centre, Milan; Cinthya Nestor, Universidad Madero, Puebla; Peter O'Connor, Musashino University, Tokyo; Cliona O'Neill, Trinity School, Rome; María José Colón Orellana, Escola Oficial d'Idiomes de Terrassa, Barcelon; Viviana Ortega, Universidad Mayor, Santiago; Luc Peeters, Kyoto Sangyo University, Kyoto; Sanja Brekalo Pelin, La Escuela Oficial de Idiomas de Coslada, Madrid; Itzel Carolina Pérez, Universidad Madero, Puebla, Mexico; Sutthima Peung, Rajamangala University of Technology Rattanakosin; Marina Pezzuoli, Liceo Scientifico Amedeo Avogadro, Rome; Andrew Pharis, Aichi Gakuin University, Nagoya; Hugh Podmore, St Giles International, UK; Carolina Porras, Universidad de La Sabana; Brigit Portilla, Colombo Americano, Cali; Soudaben Pradeep, Kaplan; Judith Puertas, Colombo Americano, Cali; Takako Ramsden, Kyoto Sangyo University, Kyoto; Sophie Rebel-Dijkstra, Aeres Hogeschool; Zita Reszler, Nottingham Language Academy, Nottingham; Sophia Rizzo, St Giles International; Gloria Stella Quintero Riveros, Universidad Catolica; Cecilia Rosas, Euroidiomas; Eleonora Salas, IICANA Centro, Córdoba; Victoria Samaniego, La Escuela Oficial de Idiomas de Pozuelo de Alarcón, Madrid; Jeanette Sandre, Universidad Madero, Puebla; Bruno Scafati, ARICANA; Anya Shaw, International House Belgrano, Argentina; Anne Smith, UNINT, Rome & University of Rome Tor Vergata, Italy; Suzannah Spencer-George, British Study Centres, Bournemouth; Students of Cultura Inglesa, São Paulo; Makiko Takeda, Aichi Gakuin University, Nagoya; Jilly Taylor, British Study Centres, London; Juliana Trisno, Kaplan, Singapore; Ruey Miin Tsao, National Cheng Kung University, Tainan City; Michelle Uitterhoeve, Vechtstede College, Weesp; Anna Maria Usai, Liceo Spallanzani, Rome; Carolina Valdiri, Colombo Americano, Cali, Colombia; Gina Vasquez, Colombo Americano, Cali; Andreas Vikran, NET School of English, Milan; Mimi Watts, Università Cattolica del Sacro Cuore, Milan; Yvonne Wee, Kaplan Higher Education Academy; Christopher Wood, Meijo University; Yanina Zagarrio, ARICANA